JO AUSTIN was born in Hamps' and sister, Jan, in Waterlooville, attended both the local Cath schools. Jo loves music and plays both ..... well as having been a member of a local band and choir. Before qualifying as a Registered Nurse, Jo worked at Cadlington House where she developed her love for children with special needs.

When her own children were born, including a son with autism, ADHD and learning difficulties, Jo decided to become a full-time mum. She continues to champion the cause of full-time devoted motherhood. Eventually returning to work when her children became adults, every job opportunity led her back to caring for children with complex needs. Now a single, mature adult, Jo is a full-time foster mum of children with additional needs. She continues to support her grown children and grandchildren. Her passion for caring is reflected in the relationships she shares with her family and her dogs.

Tug of Love

JO AUSTIN

SilverWood

Published in 2022 by SilverWood Books

SilverWood Books Ltd
14 Small Street, Bristol, BS1 1DE, United Kingdom
www.silverwoodbooks.co.uk

ISBN 978-1-80042-152-3 (paperback)
ISBN 978-1-80042-153-0 (ebook)

British Library Cataloguing in Publication Data
A CIP catalogue record for this book is
available from the British Library

Page design and typesetting by SilverWood Books

A Letter to the Reader

I hope that by sharing my story, others who suffer from mental health difficulties, for whatever reason, may find inspiration and hope within these pages.

This is my personal story. It is not meant to apportion blame or to offend anyone. Other people's recollection of events may vary and that is perfectly acceptable. I have found a forgiveness and a calm acceptance of my life and all the relationships that have intertwined and helped to make me the person I am.

I hope you enjoy my story.

Each time I visited the sink, I would wash my hands repeatedly for a count of eighty washing cycles. This became my safe number. As long as I cleaned or checked something eighty times, I might possibly accept that it was clean or safe. In other words, decontaminated.

Obsessive Compulsive Disorder, or OCD, has to be one of the most terrifying experiences ever encountered by a human being and is completely irrational. Sufferers fear that something terrible is going to happen, which is usually brought on by some deep-seated anxiety. These thoughts are called 'ruminations' and they lead to compulsive actions that people feel they must complete in order to rid themselves of the fear. For me, the compulsion was to wash my hands repeatedly. At my worst, I would visit the sink forty or fifty times during the course of the day when I thought I might be 'contaminated'.

As you can imagine, after this much washing, my hands were red raw. I washed and dried them till they bled. My hands looked like an old woman's rather than those of a young mum. For many years, I believed that this was how I was going to live the rest of my life and I couldn't cope with that. I wanted out!

My OCD fear was a very extreme and unusual form that involved a fear of colours. As you can imagine, this made it a massive problem. Every time I touched, or eventually even saw, a dreaded colour, the ruminations would begin. I don't know what I feared would happen, but I was terrified that once I was contaminated, I would spread this to my children. It got to the point where I could not touch my own children for fear of harming them. As you can see, OCD is both irrational and terrifying to those who experience it. It is an illness of the mind, like any other illness that affects parts of the body. People should not be judged or shamed for having a mental illness. It can be extremely debilitating and life-altering and it can happen to anyone. Mental health is not selective.

Many a time I sat on the back doorstep crying and begging God to take this illness away. I actually began to believe that the children and my then husband would be better off without me. I thought that my husband would be able to give the children a more normal and natural life on his own.

On two separate occasions, I tried to take my own life by overdosing on paracetamol. I am not proud of this fact. Once fully recovered, I confessed these sins to my parish priest. He blessed me and said that my sins had been absolved. I thought this would make me feel better about myself and especially about attending Mass. But in reality, I didn't feel any different. I found it difficult to go to church for many years, as I felt I didn't deserve to be in God's house. I believed I was a bad person.

Back then, I was not heavily religious, but I was baptised a Catholic and brought up in Catholic primary and secondary schools. I believed in God's teachings and although I found it difficult to be in church for a while, I still held a strong belief and I had faith and hope. I prayed to God every day.

Today, I aim to be a good person and mother. I like to think that I am trying to be as good a Christian as I can possibly be.

When I was suffering badly with OCD, I used to think the only way I would be free of the awful thoughts would be in death. I am lucky though, as I am now very much alive and mentally well, with a quiet and peaceful mind.

Perhaps I should explain how I came to be in such a low, depressed and anxious state. A little family history may help to fill in the gaps.

1

Childhood

My very earliest childhood memories are not actually of home life, but of school days, which were, for me, a far happier time. With hindsight, I think the reason for this has to be that at school there was far less criticism and condemnation compared to what I remember at home. I like to think that, actually, my teachers quite liked me.

I have very fond memories of some of my primary and secondary teachers with whom I felt I had a good bond. Despite my strict, almost controlling home life, I even formed special relationships with some of the more apparently stern, harsher characters, whom many of my peers mocked, feared or disliked. I think that's because none of them were ever as harsh as my own mother and when difficulties arose I was somehow always able to see the softer, more caring approach from even the hardest of our teachers. I learnt at a very young age how to manipulate these situations to my advantage. I don't mean to say that

I did this deliberately, more that it was a survival technique that seemed to work for me.

I'm no expert in the field of psychology, although the working of the human brain, including what happens when it goes wrong, really fascinates me. If I had my time over, or I was younger, I'd like to have trained to be a doctor specialising in psychology, helping the many people affected by problems of the mind. However, previously I didn't have the confidence to even believe this would be a possibility for me.

I believe, with all my heart, that our emotional difficulties must somehow be linked to all of our life experiences and, therefore, naturally include our very earliest experiences from the moment we not only enter this world but from the very moment of our conception. More so, I feel that our earliest memories and experiences must impact on the impression we have about the world around us, including the lessons learnt in the beginning, in the home and in our schools.

When I recall my fondest of memories regarding my teachers in both my primary and secondary schools, what's interesting to note is that I usually became most closely attached to mature, female teachers. In hindsight, I think maybe I was trying to find a warmer maternal figure who would give me the attention I craved and the warmth I needed, and I think, most importantly, encouragement. Even in my early adult life, while working as a care therapist and as a nurse, I still sought out this form of relationship in my colleagues.

Praise was something that was most definitely missing in my childhood. In fact, I think it's fair to say, there was never any praise or encouragement from my mother. There was nothing positive, only negative in the form of attention I received. It seemed to be all criticism and condemnation. I had very little attention at all from my mother, who was a businesswoman. At that time, during the sixties and seventies, this was a new breed of woman, who appeared to have little time for her family. However, as a child, I was not aware this had an impact, or that it was of any significance. Now, as a mother myself, it is easily apparent to me that what children need most, more than money or material goods, is good, quality attention.

My sister Jan and I were latch-key kids from a very young age, even in infant school. This was very unusual back in the seventies, but for us it was all we knew. So, as small children, we naturally assumed that the way we lived was the way everybody lived. We had no idea that our young friends and classmates were living much happier and more relaxed lives than ours and that in their worlds love, praise and attention were much more freely available.

Therefore, my own conclusion is that my school behaviour, although not particularly naughty – well, at least not until the later senior years – was, in fact, the behaviour of a young child craving and seeking attention – even affection. During my primary school years though, I do have very fond memories of many quite humorous events, both with my friends and teachers.

I was a bit of a cheeky little urchin, but I also think that from an early age my sense of humour and wit were quite appealing to my teachers. While being a bit cheeky and maybe a bit of a handful, I was also very eager to please and eager for praise. I did, indeed, work extremely hard because, let's face it, I didn't feel I was the smartest cookie in the tin. Certainly, my mother didn't give me credit for having any intelligence, so I believed this to be true. I worked exceptionally hard to achieve the grades I did. This was reflected in my school reports, which I have kept to this day and make for very interesting and somewhat humorous reading! What was apparent, that I see from reading them back now, was that my primary school teachers did, in fact, recognise my intelligence. They recognised hard work, determination, a willingness to please, and above all, a polite and well-mannered disposition. What more could a parent could ask for? One teacher wrote, 'Joanne works and works, just like a little beaver.' That was written when I was just six years old.

Yet I dreaded taking my school reports home. As a child, I didn't see the reports, and due to my mother's criticism, I assumed I was failing. I spent my time trying to please my mother for most of my life, desperate for her praise.

What is also interesting to note is that for a child, who was alreay recognised by teachers as having intelligence, wit and humour and, indeed, as being very 'entertaining', many of them also described a shy, sensitive and frighteningly 'anxious' child!

2

Milk Bottles and Sunday Roast

The only real memory that sticks in my mind about our first house, which we only lived in until I was six years old, is the incident with the milk bottles.

Our first house was in Greenfield Crescent in Cowplain. In those days, the milk came in glass bottles with silver foil tops and was delivered by the milkman to the front doorstep. On this occasion, there were three children in the house: me, Jan and our mum's younger brother, Tim, who was twenty years her junior, the same age as me, her younger child. Tim and I, both aged five, and Jan aged seven, being youngsters, were all up bright and early in the morning. I decided to help my mum by bringing in the milk. There were two bottles on the doorstep so I picked one up in each hand. I marched into the kitchen very triumphantly and proudly with my milk bottles. I was completely unaware that I was, in fact, holding the milk bottles upside down. As you can imagine, with the pressure of all that milk on the little silver foil tops, something had to give. As I raised the bottles with a triumphant smile to show my mum, the milk exploded through the foil tops and I, in my terror, dropped the glass bottles on the hard linoleum floor, thus adding to the mess and chaos. All three of us children froze in terror as Mum's temper, as anticipated, also exploded.

There were other adult family members in the house that day too and they have since reported that they had never, and have never since, seen three young children move so fast. To this day, I have never discovered where Jan and Tim hid that day. I spent the entire day cowering behind the old-fashioned metal dustbin in the garden. I can, at least, see the funny side of this story now because I was only trying to help and win praise. This is one of the incidents that Jan, Tim and I never discussed until recently when, I have to admit, we all had a blooming good laugh about it!

On another occasion, one Sunday lunchtime, Jan and I were waiting at the table for our lovely roast dinner, when Mum decided to have one of her meltdowns. Often these were ranting and raving, but sometimes things got thrown and even broken.

This was a particularly bad meltdown for some reason and as the roast was busy cooking in the oven, Mum decided that she was going to launch the rest of it at Dad! Veggies, potatoes, boiling water and all. How he wasn't badly hurt I'll never know.

Jan and I were about eight and six respectively and not averse to cleaning up, which we often did after such events. Not on this occasion though. Mum stormed out of the house on one of her disappearing acts (which sometimes lasted a couple of weeks by my memory) and Dad quietly began the daunting task of cleaning up the kitchen, which as I'm sure you can imagine, resembled something akin to a bombsite!

This time, Jan and I didn't venture to help. We didn't dare move from the table but merely wondered what on earth we were going to eat, as by now, our tummies were rumbling.

A while later, Dad came into the dining room and placed a bowl of gravy in front of each of us. He said something like, 'Sorry girls, that's all that's left of the dinner. Pretend it's soup!' We were both so hungry and frightened by then that we didn't dare not to eat. We also didn't dare to look up, not once – not at each other and certainly not at Dad, as we knew he was probably feeling mortified. He was such a proud man. So we just ate our 'soup' in silence.

In hindsight, I can laugh at these incidents, and you might agree that they portray quite comical scenes – although maybe that's my weird sense of humour. But, in all seriousness, the difficult situations in our childhood, for me anyway, can only be seen and discussed in a light-hearted manner and with an element of humour. It's the only way I can handle these memories. By seeing the funny side of things and laughing about it I find my mind is distracted from the truly horrible nature of the situations.

That's not to say that I don't take it all extremely seriously. As I'm sure you can imagine, for two young children to live constant-ly in a state of nervousness and fear is not a healthy way to live. Indeed, I feel that the emotional turmoil we were subjected to, for me at least, eventually led to the scars that marked my adult life with a constant cycle of ill health. At first, my mental health suffered and, after overcoming that, I spent an equally difficult time limping from one physical illness to another.

There were a couple of incidents that can never be laughed at and even I will never be able to come to terms with these events, as no child should be exposed to such atrocities early in their life.

3

Crying at the Top of the Stairs

Most of our childhood that I can clearly recollect was spent at Hurstville Drive in Waterlooville, and the one thing I remember most about that house was the staircase. I believe the houses along that street were built in the 1960s, and Jan and I were certainly sixties and seventies kids. The modern staircase was actually extremely dangerous for young children and, indeed, for dogs. It was an open-plan, highly polished, wooden staircase. Needless to say, we had several mishaps on these stairs, but what I remember most was that if you sat at the very top of the stairs you could hear everything in the entire house, even behind closed doors.

Many a night, when supposedly in bed, Jan and I would creep out of our room and sit at the top of the stairs listening to the barrage of seemingly endless, violent, verbal abuse that our mother would throw at our father. Jan, being the elder by two years, would always put her arm around my shoulders and try her hardest to comfort me as I cried.

I adored my dad and hated that Mum constantly hurt him. I know Dad wasn't the easiest of people to live with – tell me someone who is – but I had so much respect for him. Although stern and old-fashioned and a very proud and private person, when the chips were down, for Jan and me especially, in both childhood and adulthood, he never let us down. He was always there for us. Even if he thought we were in the wrong, he would still support us, unconditionally.

Dad was a very quiet man who said little and showed little emotion; he certainly never seemed to like discussing serious issues. He was also an extremely intelligent man despite, as he called it, his inadequate education. Dad had to leave school at fourteen to work on a farm in order to support his own parents and siblings, but he taught himself practically everything. He was one of those people who could turn his hand to anything and everything; he even kept up with technology. He became a self-taught computer whizz kid in his seventies! He was well respected among the whole family, but especially by me. I loved Dad to bits. We all used to say, 'If it's broke, Dad'll fix it!'

It is probably fair to say, however, that parenting didn't come naturally to Dad, but he always did his best. He made an even more amazing effort with his grandchildren, and they worshipped him. What he did do made up for what was missing in other relationships though. He provided warmth, stability, safety, consistency, nurturing, affection, attention, love and presence. He was completely unaware that he was providing us with our safe base and our secure haven. Things I was to discover later, as a foster parent, that are essential for children to thrive.

Dad did, at least, bring us up to be extremely polite and respectful to all people; you could say we were brought up too well. I, and Jan especially, find it very difficult to intentionally hurt another person's feelings, even unintentionally for that matter. My sister is actually so nice, she always sees the best in people and situations, and also never has a bad word to say. I do try to follow her example, but I, unfortunately, am the wilder and more impulsive one of the two of us.

I'm unsure whether or not it was the crying at the top of the stairs that started it, but one night, when Jan was around nine years old, she began sleepwalking. Her bedroom was nearest to the top of the stairs, so these events prompted a need for a change in sleeping arrangements. We had to swap bedrooms. I was heartbroken because, being the youngest, I had the smallest box bedroom at the end of the hallway. I loved my little bedroom and always felt safe and secure there, alone in my own tiny room. I spent many happy hours there soothing myself by cuddling my favourite toy. This was Pilly, the pillow I'd had since being a baby. Being suddenly uprooted into a much bigger bedroom with so much vast, empty space was quite frightening, but I knew that Jan needed to be protected, so I didn't protest. How she never fell down the stairs is a miracle too. I was so happy when all this passed and I was finally reunited with my own little bedroom. Even as a child though, I would have done anything to protect *my* Jan, although I wouldn't have admitted it at the time, of course.

Now, along with my own family and Dad, I love Jan the most in the entire world. There is a saying about sisters that goes, 'Growing up together made us special friends forever!' Jan *is* my best friend. We've shared so much together and she's still the most kind-hearted, thoughtful, loving person you could ever wish to meet. You couldn't find a better person who is always so jolly. I often wonder if behind that smile, there may be a very tormented soul, but she'll never let it show. Like Dad, she rarely discusses serious issues but glosses over them or changes the subject.

Since finally sharing my memories of our childhood with Jan, she simply says she doesn't remember any of it. I'm sure I didn't imagine any of it or make it up. Other family members certainly discuss those times with me and share the same memories. Jan shared recently that she understands that her way of coping with it is that she doesn't want to remember. Maybe if she doesn't remember, then to her it didn't happen. We all have different coping mechanisms. I wouldn't want to ever upset her so I accept that's her way and I have to be respectful of that. My way, however, is to talk about it all and get it off my chest. I have a couple of aunties who are great confidantes and I discuss things with them. Sometimes my way of coping is to tell family stories with a sprinkling of cheeky wit and humour. I often wonder if Jan is much better at coping than I am.

4

The Christmas from Hell

One of the most traumatic events for me personally as a young child was the Christmas Eve of the year I was seven years old. Mum and Dad both worked at the old Post Office Telephone Exchange in Cosham at that time, Dad as a telephone engineer and Mum as one of the original telephone operators. Mum often worked evenings or night shifts, I think to fit around Dad's work and us children. This particular Christmas Eve, Mum was working the evening shift at the telephone exchange, so Dad had taken me and Jan to spend the evening with Nan and Midge. This was one of my favourite ways to spend time anyway, so I was more than delighted with the arrangement.

On the way home in the car, around 11pm or midnight, Dad was driving us around the Cosham roundabout when he spotted Mum's car. Sitting beside her in the car was a man whom we had not seen before. Dad responded in such a way as Jan and I had never previously witnessed. We had never seen our father angry and he had certainly never been an aggressive man, not in any measure. So this proved to be a very difficult evening as our dad, totally out of character, began to curse and swear. Unusually, I can't recall the words he used in the car (I usually recall actions and conversations with detailed accuracy), but I do recall that he drove round and round this roundabout chasing Mum's car a bit like a mad man. Both cars eventually pulled into the layby and dad shot out of the car, dragged the man from Mum's car and a fight began. I was so scared. I'd never witnessed anything like this and even at seven years old I began to guess that Mum should not have been with this man, nor was this a relationship that should have been going on. The next moment was the biggest shock of all, as Dad shoved the man's head through my open window, shouting, 'Say hello to your new father!' I think I screamed. I was certainly trembling and crying. I don't remember how the altercation ended, but I recall Dad driving us back to Nan's house with Mum in hot pursuit. At Nan's, I ran inside and hid behind my nan, as Dad and Mum engaged in an almighty shouting match. I whispered to Nan, 'Don't let her get me.' I don't know what I thought would happen, but I wanted to stay with my nan. Somehow though, we all ended up back at home where Jan and I were ushered to bed. Needless to say, we didn't remain in our beds but returned to one of our frequent nightly vigils at the top of the stairs as the angry, abusive comments continued into the night.

Next day, Christmas Day, I wondered how the day might be. Surprisingly though, both Mum and Dad behaved as though nothing at all had happened the night before. Dad even gave Mum a diamond eternity ring for her Christmas present. I remember thinking how strange all this was. Even at seven years old I'd begun to work out that this was not a normal way to be behaving in family relationships. I particularly remember thinking what a strange gift for Dad to give Mum when she had clearly done something that was not good at all. I also thought how false the whole scene appeared and felt very uncomfortable with it.

This was a quiet Christmas and my saddest family memory. Days later, as I walked through the shopping precinct with my dad, and as we were about to cross the road, Dad took my hand. I looked up at him and said, 'If you and Mum ever split up, I want to stay with you forever.' I also remember that I then realised that this was a very strange and sad comment for a seven-year-old to make to her father.

Humour aside, to be fair to Mum, I am seriously trying to recall happy memories of that time but am sadly finding this difficult. In all honesty, if I remember correctly, the happiest times were when Jan and I were left alone in the house or, for me, when I spent quality time on my own with Dad. Much excitement also came with the promise of a visit to Nan and Midge. (That's our dad's mum and his sister, who always lived together until Nan passed away). Nan and Midge spent a lot of what I call 'quality time' with me and Jan. Some would call it being spoilt rotten, but what are grandparents for? Aunties too? I adored Nan and Midge, which meant that the six-week summer holidays spent with them for many a year, while our parents both worked, were the highlight of my year.

I didn't get to spend as much time as I'd have liked with my nan, but she was the most naturally spontaneous, loving and tender person I had known and I decided that when I had children and grandchildren of my own I wanted to make sure I was just like her. I would love to have talked about my childhood with her, to share this book with her – in fact, share all of my life with her. Sadly, Nan passed away when I was nineteen, but I know she's always watching over me and would be extremely proud of her grandchildren, and her great-grandchildren, especially after all the turmoil that Jan and I went through as youngsters. Considering that, I think we've both turned out pretty well.

When Nan passed away, I still hadn't worked out for myself why I was such a wild yet vulnerable person. I think Nan probably knew all that had happened, even the incidents she hadn't witnessed. She was a very wise person. I did, however, discuss our childhood with Midge. She says that, despite everything, I was always quite a humorous, wild, tomboyish kind of a girl. She recalls one occasion at Nan's house, when I was amusing the entire family with my antics and, with everybody laughing at me, Nan apparently stood up in the middle of the room and said, 'You may laugh at her now, but she'll go far she will.' I think Nan also believed in the supernatural and maybe even had some psychic powers. Maybe she just always knew I'd be OK.

Apart from my parents, Nan and Midge were the most influential people in shaping and modelling my personality in my early years.

5

Mum Leaving Home

I had, unfortunately, been caught smoking at school. I was, after all, always seeking attention and always in with the wrong crowd, not to mention, at the age of thirteen, a bit of a rebel too. As many of the teachers at our school were nuns, smoking was quite a shocking misdemeanour. To make matters worse, it was Sister Ruth-Mary who had to deal with me. She was my form tutor by then, but she was also my friend. She remained so throughout my adult years, even visiting me in St James' Hospital when I was very poorly. But in those days, my peers and I referred to her, some of us more affectionately than others, as Mini Batman or the Caped Crusader, as her habit flew along behind her as she bustled through the school corridors.

Sister Ruth-Mary had watched me grow since I was a tiny tot when Mum used to take us to Mass at the school chapel. The sisters would observe us silently from the back pews. Jan and I would sit prim and proper, not daring to say a word, not because we were listening and taking in the knowledge being taught, but through fear of a clip behind the ears from Mum if we dared to breathe, let alone move or speak. I would be suitably dressed, with my long brown plaits trailing down my back. When it was time for the priest to sign my permission slip for transferring to the senior school, Sister Ruth-Mary was present and made the dreadful mistake of telling me that she hoped I'd be as good as my big sister. Well, that had done it. I knew I could in no way live up to the academic or behavioural ideals my sister had set, so I decided there and then that I'd have to get myself known in my own right by being the exact opposite. That's how it began – my crusade of 'respectful' disobedience and mischief within my senior school career. I would never truly upset the nuns, as I had the greatest of respect and admiration for them, but I had to make my mark, didn't I?

The day she caught me smoking, Sister Ruth-Mary took me aside. She explained that knowing how honest I was, and knowing my mum, she would give me time to get home and explain my involvement in the smoking incident to my mum quietly myself before she would phone and speak with her. She explained that it would be much better for me and Mum if I brought the subject up first and prepared my mum for the nun's telephone call.

Well, of course, that is what I did. I told my mum, very quietly, that I had something to tell her and there unfolded my confession. Did Sister Ruth-Mary ever phone my mum? No! She knew me too well. She knew that I might have been a mischief-maker but that I was also very honest, reliable and fair. I could have got away with keeping quiet, but no, I did the right thing.

What followed was not at all what I had expected either though. I expected shouting, ranting and raving, telling me how much I'd let everyone down, followed by a severe punishment. Instead, Mum said, 'Get your coat. We're going to the chippie.' I was so confused. As we drove through town, Mum then spoke quietly but sternly. I didn't like this version of reprimand; I'd have felt more comfortable with what I was used to.

Shockingly, she came straight out with, 'If you think you're old enough to smoke, then I think you're old enough to know that I'm going to leave your father.' I was dumbfounded. I remember thinking, 'I only tried one cigarette!' She continued to explain that she wouldn't leave him yet, and she would wait until after my O levels. I thought, OK. What else could I think? At least there was the consolation that she would be around for another three or four years. No more was said; we got fish and chips and went home.

That was on a Friday afternoon. On the following Monday morning, Sister Ruth-Mary asked me if I'd spoken to my mum. I nodded. She smiled, and no more was said.

That very same Monday afternoon, only three days after Mum's conversation with me, as I opened the front door, returning from school, I noticed that Mum's prize rubber plant was missing from its spot in the hallway. It was nowhere near time for my O levels, but I knew exactly what this meant. Mum had gone! I wasn't so much sad that she'd left but devastated that she hadn't asked me if I wanted to go with her. Not that I would have gone with her anyway. I'd always said that I'd stay with my dad and that hadn't changed. What I felt, though, was that she'd abandoned me. I thought I may have been to blame and that I must be a pretty bad person if my own mother didn't want me. She didn't leave her beautiful rubber plant behind yet she chose to leave me! I guess that's just how children think. Perhaps that was when my low self-esteem truly began. Believe it or not, that was the easier part. Next came the letter from Mum to Dad.

The act of Mum leaving the family home after years of threatening to go, in reality held few emotions for me other than feeling devastation and pity for my father. It was I, at the age of thirteen, who held him as he sobbed and sobbed when he read the note she had left him. As a young teenage girl, I had no idea how much emotion a man could hold in his heart and I certainly had no idea how to console him. I remember him crying uncontrollably for hours and I just hugged him. I felt so desperate for him and somewhat surprised too, because, for my own part, the only emotions I was feeling were relief and acceptance. You might think these very unusual emotions for a girl to be experiencing when her mother has just left home.

When Dad finally stopped crying, we both realised that teatime had long since come and gone, and we were both feeling a little light-headed with hunger. Dad simply said, 'We'd better go get some fish and chips then.' We never mentioned the evening again, but fish and chip suppers became a common and welcome treat that we often shared to celebrate good events or commiserate over the not-so-good ones.

Would you believe though that very early in our lives Jan and I thought this was how every family lived? We thought this was all perfectly normal until we got a bit older and started visiting friends without our parents. What a different picture we saw!

Dad cared for me and supported me through the teenage years until I left home at sixteen to live at my place of work, a lovely children's home for severely disabled children. I lived and played with my work colleagues and thoroughly enjoyed my work. I was in my element, happy as Larry, so to speak.

I remained thus for five years. The only major upset in this time was my lovely nan passing when I was nineteen. I was heartbroken; I grieved for quite some time. When the grief passed, I decided to train as a nurse. Following my passion to care for others but to gain a formal qualification at the same time would set me on a good career path, or so I thought. Dad still continued to be my biggest supporter and was always there when I needed someone.

I continued in nursing for a year after qualifying. I was a staff nurse on the renal unit and yet again I loved what I was doing. Marriage and my own family followed and I chose to be a full-time mum. I wanted to be the mother and grandmother that Nanny Moores had been. I wanted my children to have all the love and encouragement that I could possibly give. Not criticism or condemnation but praise, affection, love and encouragement in abundance. Little did I know that doing so without support from those I loved and who should have been there for me would lead to so much illness and heartache. My father, my sister and my aunts continued to support me unconditionally with my young family. It was the ones who should have been there but failed to provide the love, affection and support expected, such as my husband and mother, who I think probably caused such feelings of low self-esteem and lack of self-worth. It was to be many years before I would work out and accept this realisation.

6

Becoming a Family

I met my husband on a skiing holiday in Andorra. Within a year, we were married, on a beautiful day in May 1989. Just one year later, we started our young family with Jennifer Elizabeth, born on 16 August 1990 on a wonderfully hot summer's day. Jennifer's entrance into the world was just the icing on the cake. She was bonnie and bright and filled our lives with love and happiness.

When Jennifer was just five months old, I fell pregnant again. The sadness that followed the unfortunate loss of that baby at eight weeks pregnant was unbearable, but I had Jennifer to keep me going.

After this loss, it proved difficult for me to conceive again, but eventually we found ourselves preparing for the joyful arrival of our second child, Robert John, born on 27 May 1992. Robert was a complete surprise to family, friends and ourselves, as after a history of ten baby girls in the family we had naturally

29

expected this baby to be yet another girl.

Once Jennifer and Robert were settled in their respective schools, we welcomed the somewhat hasty arrival of baby number three, a second girl. We were once again delighted and we called her Catherine Sarah. She was born on 4 February 1995.

I don't imagine there is one mother or father who cannot remember the midwife's words upon delivery of their beautiful, precious child. The words, 'It's a girl' or 'It's a boy', have to be the most amazing words one ever utters to another human being. Certainly, in my case this was very true.

I will never forget the magical birth of all of my children. Each was wonderful and precious. What a great gift to be presented with such perfect, tiny miracles. Needless to say, my family were delighted with the news of my second pregnancy, and having one daughter already, the usual response was, 'Let's hope for a boy this time'. I have to admit, secretly I still hoped for another girl. I was only used to girls and had only ever dealt with baby girls. The thought of having two little girls of my own was wonderful. I had no idea what little boys were like and am now totally ashamed to think that I would rather not have had one, thank you very much!

However, God saw fit, in 1992, to present me with a baby boy. I thank God for ignoring my prayers for another girl (yes, I really did pray for a girl). In the delivery room, when the midwife said those amazing words, 'It's a boy', my immediate thoughts were not quite as negative as I had expected. I actually remember thinking, 'He's born. He's alive. He's healthy and he's mine.' It didn't really matter what sex he was, although my very next thought was how on earth was I going to react to a baby boy? I didn't give it another thought because the very next moment my baby boy was in my arms and I fell in love with him immediately. Total, unconditional love was the only, overwhelming feeling.

I don't know who was more surprised about the birth of my baby boy, my family or me, because, although they had all hoped it would be a boy, they had assumed, as I had, it would be another girl.

I must just add at this point that, after that wondrous moment, my sister was also blessed with a baby boy, after her first-born had also been a girl. I thank God for allowing her to share with me the joy of having children of both sexes. What a wonderful life experience!

Having revelled in my baby boy, it's not to say I love my girls any less. Now I am happy to say that I love girls and I love boys. They may certainly be slightly different ways of loving, but the love is always divided equally between my children.

My baby boy soon became the apple of everybody's eyes. He, in turn, rewarded us a thousand times over with an abundance of love and affection, this being attributed to his being a little boy. His cup was indeed overflowing.

7

Robert's First Year

I cannot pretend that the first year with Robert was an easy one, far from it. However, having already had one child, Jennifer, who was twenty-one months old when Robert was born, and realising just how quickly they grow and change, I was determined I was going to enjoy his first year.

When I first knew I was pregnant again, I decided that this time round, I would breastfeed. I had always felt guilt and a pang of regret about the decision not to breastfeed Jennifer. However, I was young and naive, and to be honest, the thought of breastfeeding wasn't appealing. To placate my guilt, I convinced myself that if I breastfed Jennifer when I didn't want to, my tension and stress would be transmitted to her. This, in turn, would probably mean it wouldn't work, and then I would have to change over to bottle-feeding midway – even more upheaval for the baby. Probably my reticence to breastfeed Jennifer was linked to my lack of confidence, and

I had decided I'd fail even before giving it a go.

Added to all of these feelings was the fact that we also happened to be moving house the very week that Jennifer was born, so for all these reasons at the time, rightly or wrongly, I chose to bottle-feed and thought I was doing the right thing. Jennifer, in fact, turned out to be a wonderful baby, a real pleasure and a textbook baby. She fed regularly at three-hour intervals; she slept well during the day and night and was quite a bundle of fun.

I recovered quickly from Jennifer's birth. I wasn't tired and I enjoyed my baby. We were, however, spoilt by all this, as Jennifer slept through the night after just five weeks. She reached all the milestones ahead of schedule and presented as an Ideal Baby. Maybe some of this was just me trying too hard to get it all right and do it all by the book. When Jennifer was about six weeks old though, I began to feel I hadn't done it right at all. I thought I hadn't given her my best; I felt then that I should at least have tried to breastfeed her.

Thus, when Robert was born, armed with all this new information, regrets and guilt, together with an undying determination to get it all right second time around, I knew I was going to breastfeed Robert successfully because I felt so positive about it. I guess I also thought that at least there was nothing else for me to learn, as I'd done the rest before.

This positive attitude and sheer determination won and did the trick; the breastfeeding was quickly and easily established. I found myself surprised to be saying that I actually enjoyed breastfeeding. What a shame I hadn't been more encouraged the first time round. It really was a pleasant feeling feeding my son.

I loved all the cuddling and the closeness we felt and the bonding was wonderful. The sheer dependence and intimacy of those moments was a marvel. I can't, however, paint a picture of total harmony and perfection here, though, as there were times when, after seemingly feeding the baby for hours on end and feeling totally and utterly exhausted, I would long for sleep. I would rest my head on the pillow, feeling that sleep was imminent and Robert would wake, crying to be fed again. I am sure many mothers at these times have thought, 'I cannot feed you any more today. Please, just let me sleep a while.'

I very quickly noticed this amazing difference between breastfeeding and bottle-feeding. I was exhausted!

Had Robert been my first baby, maybe I wouldn't have noticed this so much, as I could have rested more when he slept. However, already having one very energetic, enthusiastic and extremely inquisitive toddler to look after as well did add up to double trouble.

Although the feeling of breastfeeding was wonderful, Robert never seemed to settle much past the initial two hours. Again, in hindsight, perhaps I shouldn't have given in so much to him. Maybe he really didn't need feeding all those times, but Robert seemed to be an extremely sensitive, restless baby. Looking back now, it's easy to see why, but at the time, in my ignorance, I just did my best.

Robert only ever seemed to respond to the stimulus of being held, touched, cuddled and above all nursed at the breast. Luckily, having decided that I was going to enjoy his first year, I relaxed a bit more than I had with Jennifer. I let the house go a little bit more and devoted myself to trying to be a good mummy and giving him as much attention as he wanted in the early months. Some may say I was guilty of overindulging and spoiling him, but luckily, as it turns out, he really did need this, and thankfully, I now have no regrets about the attention I gave him.

I gave him my best when he needed me most and it also helped me to recognise that it didn't matter that I hadn't breastfed Jennifer, because she too had her share of attention, cuddles and love as a baby. I realised that at the time I did what I felt was right for her and that she too had our devotion, but in a slightly different way. In fact, she had the devotion of the entire family as Daddy and Gran also enjoyed feeding her and holding her close as a tiny baby. They too had shared in that feeling of dependence and devotion.

Robert seemed to be quite a demanding baby and after four months I gave up breastfeeding him, hoping that I might feel less exhausted and that he for once might settle better and we might even get a good night's sleep. There had been no physical problems with the breastfeeding, such as mastitis, sore or cracked nipples, engorgement or anything. I felt it had all come quite naturally. I had a good milk supply, Robert latched on beautifully and we were both enjoying it. So I felt a little disappointed giving up, and found it a difficult decision to make. I remember thinking at the time, 'I love having babies and I love breastfeeding. I hope I can have another baby because I want to do this all again.'

Bottle-feeding didn't go quite as I expected, either. But again, we were unaware at the time that Robert had any problems. We found out at ten months old that his tonsils and adenoids were huge, but at the time of changing from breast to bottle I became very frustrated that feeding time, which was supposed to be a pleasant experience, was turning into something to dread. I had assumed that Robert would have a good feed and settle contentedly after the formula milk. I had imagined we would still be close and loving at feed time. Instead, Robert would cough and splutter and one or other of us, usually both, would end up wearing most of the milk.

Robert still didn't sleep through the night and still didn't settle too well, but I convinced myself it would get better. I actually put most of Robert's behaviour down to the fact that he was a boy and that he was a second child. I had often been told that boys are slower than girls and that the second child doesn't always reach milestones as quickly as their sibling. I quite naively thought he was just a lazy, sensitive boy. I must admit, I didn't watch for milestones and every achievement in quite the same way as I had with Jennifer, but again I thought I shouldn't expect him to be as advanced as she was. Who, these days, has time to watch out for all these things when one has two young children, living as we do at such a pace in today's stressful society?

Imagine our surprise, therefore, when at eight months old, Robert had his development test and failed to respond to any of the sounds used for the hearing checks! I remember the health visitor saying, 'Never mind, he probably has a cold. We'll check again in a few weeks' time when he's feeling better.' A few weeks later, when we returned for the hearing checks, Robert seemed quite well but again he failed to respond to any of the sounds. I don't know who was more surprised, the health visitor or me. We looked at each other with total disbelief. I felt quite shocked as she said she would refer him to the clinic for a full hearing test.

Shortly after this, Robert had a chest infection, one of many in his first year. This time, he seemed bluer than usual round the lips and was really struggling for breath. I called the doctor and he was rushed into hospital with upper-airways obstruction. This was partly due to the fact that he had a chest infection but also due to him having very large tonsils and adenoids, which exacerbated the problem. We had guessed by this time

36

that Robert's tonsils and adenoids would have to be removed at some point, but we had not appreciated the effect this was also having on his hearing. Robert was monitored overnight while in hospital, given Ventolin nebulisers and we left the following day without realising that Robert was also seriously asthmatic.

The appointment for Robert's hearing test came through quite quickly, much to our relief, but again Robert performed quite poorly. Although not totally deaf, he had very little hearing. My husband and I had still not put two and two together and made the connection with his large tonsils. How very pathetic of me, you might say, as I had in fact trained as a nurse myself and worked many times in the ear, nose and throat wards! I can assure you that no amount of training in childcare, nursing or raising children prepares you for your own offspring's health problems. Far from it. In fact, sometimes I think a little knowledge can do more harm than good. We imagined all sorts of things could be wrong with Robert; emotions took over and common sense didn't stand a chance.

8

Silent Panic

After the hearing test, I remember the audiologist saying he would refer Robert to the ear, nose and throat specialist. He told us we would receive the appointment through the post, and sent us off home, telling us to be patient.

I cried throughout the whole afternoon; there were many more tears for Robert over the years. I remember thinking, 'What if he never hears me tell him I love him.'

It seemed like an eternity before he saw the ENT consultant, but we were lucky, as he was actually seen two weeks later in an emergency clinic. The consultant, as we expected, said she would remove Robert's tonsils and adenoids and, at the same time, put grommets in his ears. The penny dropped and suddenly I felt stupid; of course, his hearing would improve once his tonsils and adenoids were removed and his ears were drained with grommets.

The consultant said she would perform surgery as soon as

Robert was fit enough for an operation, as the problems with his tonsils and adenoids were making his life a misery; he was still having difficulty feeding and breathing. We went away feeling quite high. Our emotions had been up and down like yo-yos for some time. We thought that the end was in sight and that any day now Robert would have his operation and all would be well.

However, Robert wasn't going to let us off the hook that easily. He then suffered infection after infection and it seemed he was never going to be fit enough for surgery. A time did come, however, when for all intents and purposes, he seemed quite fit and well. We were given a date two weeks later and prepared ourselves for D-Day.

Of course, looking back now, it all makes sense why Robert was so restless as a baby and why he only responded to cuddling, touching and nursing frequently. He didn't respond to the sound of voices and I hadn't even noticed. How ashamed I felt that I had missed this. Everyone tried to reassure me that you don't notice as much with your second baby as your first, but as his mother I felt that I should have noticed these things. It's just a good job I did give in to his demands to be loved and cuddled all the time. I have no regrets about that. He needed me and, luckily, I responded as naturally as I believed I could.

We made arrangements for the operation day. Jennifer went to stay with her gran for a few days and I prepared overnight bags for Robert and myself. We had been advised to allow two days in hospital: the day of the operation and the following day to check all was well. I already had images of this perfectly healthy, happy, hearing baby boy that I would bring home, although at the same time I was, of course, very emotional about my baby having an operation and anaesthetic.

From the moment I left him in the anaesthetic room, he was no longer totally dependent on me. We had to hand over our baby to the doctors and trust in them completely, something I found very hard to come to terms with. I cried as I walked away from him asleep in that room. He looked so small and vulnerable that I wanted pick him up in my arms and run away with him. But I knew deep down he needed the operation to improve his quality of life, so who was I to deny him that? We felt like emotional wrecks.

The anaesthetist was not completely convinced that Robert was fit enough for the operation but like us thought we would never catch him in a much better condition. So he agreed to proceed with the operation. Having seen many doctors over the course of the year, with Robert's repeated chest infections and feeding problems, I was amazed this was the first doctor who agreed with me that there was something not quite right about Robert but said he couldn't put his finger on what it was. I think he felt a little dubious or uneasy about the whole thing. What I am saying to all of you parents who have been in this situation is to stand by your instincts; Mum really does know best!

I had been saying for a long time that Robert was far more poorly than anyone else was prepared to believe. I even convinced myself that I was being neurotic, and was sure that was what most doctors thought of me too. I began to play things down and reassured myself that soon it would all be over. All these thoughts were going through my mind as I waited for the time to pass. The nurse had said, 'He'll be back on the ward in just forty minutes.' I had convinced myself that after the operation that would be the end of all these problems.

Forty minutes came and went; in fact, an hour came and

went. Other children were returning from their operations, but there was still no sign of my Robert. I looked at Mike, who in turn was looking at his watch again and looking very worried. I didn't speak as I struggled to resist the silent panic rising inside of me. I kept telling myself everything was OK, and he would be back in a minute.

A nurse popped her head round the door and disappeared again. I heard her in the corridor outside as she said, 'Yes, they are in here. Shall I call them?' She returned to the room and said, 'Don't panic, but the doctor would like to see you in the operating suite.'

I remember thinking what a funny thing to say. Of course we were panicking. Why couldn't she just tell us what was wrong? Of course, she couldn't tell us because she didn't know; she just knew there was a problem and was told to fetch us.

In a state of complete panic, I couldn't accept this. I thought the nurse couldn't tell us because Robert was dead and she wanted the doctor to tell us. How silly of me. Did I honestly think the doctor would make us walk down that long, long corridor to the operating suite to learn the worst? Obviously, the nurse didn't realise the tricks your mind plays during times of such stress. Of course, if Robert had been dead, the doctor would have come to us.

I was so relieved to find that my baby was alive, but I still couldn't stop crying. I cried all the way down that long corridor. I had walked down that corridor so many times as a nurse, but as a mother it was the longest walk I'd ever taken in the world. By the time I reached the doctor, I was shaking and felt I was losing control. I told myself to get a grip, sort myself out and get some composure; we needed to understand what the doctor was telling us.

The doctor explained that Robert had suffered an asthma attack while under the anaesthetic and that his right lung had collapsed. She said that they were ventilating him and that he was being taken to intensive care, as he would require artificial ventilation. As I started to cry again, she became the firm but gentle doctor I remembered her to be from working with her some years earlier. She reminded me that I knew this was for the best and that they would have everything under control. She also added that they would always be totally honest with us.

It was going to be some time apparently before they would be ready for Robert in intensive care, and under normal circumstances it would have been some time before we could see him. However, thankfully, the doctor quickly realised that I would find more reassurance if I could see Robert immediately. She was right. The doctor led me into the operating theatre. Robert's little body lay on what appeared at the time to be a hideously large bed for this tiny baby; it was, in fact, the operating table. He was so still and looked so pale, and there were tubes everywhere. As a nurse, I should have been more prepared for this, but again, when it's your own child lying there, emotions play havoc with you and certainly don't give your brain a chance.

Robert looked so alone and vulnerable and I felt so hopeless. I couldn't pick him up and run away with him, which is what I wanted to do, so I kissed him and whispered, 'Mummy loves you. See you in a bit.' At least by now I felt more reassured that he was alive, and where there's life there's hope!

We sat in the lounge outside intensive care as they settled Robert in and prepared for us to see him. Mike phoned the family to explain what had happened and the nurse phoned for the hospital chaplain to come and sit with us as we had requested. The chaplain happened to be a family friend and had officiated at our marriage. Thankfully, his new job was that of hospital chaplain. Frequently over the next few horrific days, he sat with us, and even made the tea for us when Jennifer came to visit with Gran. He tried hard to maintain some kind of normality for the whole family. He needn't have said a word in all that time; his presence alone was reassuring and comforting. Having a friend like him around made me feel that I almost had a shortcut to God. It was as though I had jumped the queue with Him to get my prayers answered, because I had this helping hand up the ladder, so to speak!

And goodness, did we pray! So many people prayed for Robert. My family, Mike's family, our church, Mike's mum's church, the chaplain and many other people who heard about him. God probably thought he'd better sort this out as he was getting earache!

Along with other members of the family, Jan, my sister, was also there to support me and it wasn't until writing this that we talked about that time. I hadn't realised how upset she was too. She recalled that when she first came into intensive care, and saw Robert attached to all of the tubes, all she kept thinking was that she mustn't cry, because she didn't want to upset me. I in turn was thinking of her, visiting her nephew in this condition, because at the time she was three months pregnant with her baby boy. Despite all we were going through, we were still thinking of each other. Just being together was all the comfort we needed; words are not always necessary.

It's strange to think I didn't ask God to make him better than he was before the operation, just to let him live. In fact, at that moment, when he was on the ventilator, I wasn't even sure if the operation was finished. I didn't even know how far in the operation they had gone before they ran into problems. I remember the doctor saying at least his tonsils were in the bin; they really had needed to come out. I wasn't sure though if they had managed to get the grommets in and didn't care. I would rather have him not hearing than not have him at all! I vowed that he would never have another operation, unless it was a question of life or death. Maybe that's selfish. Would he thank me when he was a bit older if his hearing was not very good and was affecting his quality of life? Well, I didn't know. That was something to worry about if the problem arose, certainly not at that point.

I just thanked God for answering our prayers. Robert recovered and was taken off the ventilator after three days and remained in intensive care for a further twenty-four hours to ensure he could maintain his breathing on his own. I'm not sure where people get the strength from at times like these, but I remained at his side while he was in intensive care and had very little sleep. We were given a little room nearby, furnished with a couple of camp beds so we could get some rest, but I just couldn't leave him. I remained by his side. I stayed at the hospital with Robert for a further three days on the ward while he recovered. He had frequent Ventolin nebulisers and antibiotics. He began to eat again and gradually improved in his general health.

Robert started to smile, laugh and amuse everyone again, but he still slept little at night and I was exhausted. The family came in often to keep me company and take him for walks in his pram, and generally tried to give me a break. I finally left his side to go home to Mum's – we had a more reconciled relationship when I became a mother – for a bath, a rest and a decent meal. I stayed away for a full two hours before I felt compelled to return to his side.

I have to mention the nurse who cared for Robert from the moment he entered intensive care. I remember thinking how difficult it must have been for the nurse looking after him, and particularly after I discovered that she herself had a baby exactly the same age as Robert. How must she have felt looking after one so young, like her own and yet so poorly? She coped and responded very well indeed. She was extremely professional. Later on, when Robert was recovering, she told me that she had struggled hard to fight back the tears when she let me in to see him for the first time on the ventilator. She said she found that quite difficult because obviously she could imagine exactly what I must be feeling. All I can say is that she was wonderful. I thanked her gratefully for taking such good care of my son.

After another week we were allowed to take Robert home. I thanked God for my son, and our young family.

9

A Word about Discipline

Robert was eleven and a half months old when he had his operation. It was his first birthday the week after he was allowed home. We had not really planned a party, but after the ordeal we had all been through we decided to celebrate. We invited everyone to share with us: family, friends, neighbours and all the children. It was wonderful.

My mum bought Robert a Noddy car, one of those pedal-along ones. She tied ribbons and balloons on it and we all watched the sheer delight as Robert was shown his new toy. I will never forget the smile on his face that day. I don't think he stopped smiling all day and neither did we. It seemed hard to believe that day just how poorly he had been only a couple of weeks before.

Robert's general health improved rapidly over the following year. He was diagnosed as asthmatic and we had to give him Ventolin inhalers with a mask over his face when he had an attack. These were quite frequent and frightening when he had just come home from hospital. He didn't like the mask, but it made him better. The attacks lessened and he seemed to grow out of it, with attacks as frequent as once a year eventually.

Along with his improved health, Robert started to talk; just one word at a time but definitely words. In fact, in the first few months, we were so excited as he seemed to copy so many words so quickly. Then he came to a standstill again. We knew he should be progressing on to two words together and more, but it didn't happen. People kept telling us to be patient, but Robert was now beginning to get frustrated and we were feeling a little disappointed again.

We tried all the usual things, talking slowly and deliberately to him and pronouncing each word clearly, but he seemed to get even more frustrated. I think he knew there should be something more. I don't think we were stupid parents by any means; we really did try for Robert, but he just reverted to pointing at things and saying 'UGH!' for what he wanted. We tried not giving him what he wanted, such as a drink, for example, unless he spoke the word and maybe even 'please', but it just seemed to make him worse. Robert started to have many tantrums and his behaviour seemed so erratic. There were good periods when he seemed quite calm and tried hard and then there would be times when he regressed and his behaviour would be quite unpredictable.

I must admit that when he first came home from hospital, I seemed to be somewhat lacking in my approach to discipline with both the children. I was so glad to have them that I found it very difficult to say no to either of them! Needless to say, eventually, with the children getting their own way all the time, things began to get out of control. Jennifer, especially, had been

47

pretty well disciplined from the moment she was born and was the type of child who needs very firm boundaries. She needed to know exactly where she stood, exactly what was or was not acceptable and just how far she could push you. In fact, I think this is fair to say of most children. They need to have very clear boundaries set, and Jennifer was the type of child that if you give her an inch, she takes a mile!

Very quickly, (well, after a month or so) we understood that we were going to have to show more control and confidence in order to regain some degree of normality. I realised that we were spoiling the children, that to give in to their every whim does not in fact prove to them how much you love them. Discipline is important for everyone. Indeed, we were not doing them any favours at all. I, especially, was guilty of gross overindulgence and of depriving my children of important knowledge and experience of what is right and wrong and of how to grow and learn with a healthy attitude.

We started with the basics: getting back to normal mealtimes; not picking between meals; sitting at the table to eat and drink; not wandering around the house with food or drinks; and getting back to normal bedtimes. These were all things we had been consistent with before, but as I've already mentioned, our discipline had grown lax. Children need structure and routine, and I thought we had always been quite good at these, so I was surprised to find myself feeling guilty if I didn't give in to them. However, after reading an excellent article about discipline, it gave me the strength to stick to my guns and be firm or gentle, but to discipline appropriately when I felt it was needed.

Children need to learn that love is spoken through the word 'no' as much as 'yes'. I am a firm believer in this teaching and that, in fact, not to discipline one's children is, in truth, proof of neglect rather than love. A child who grows up believing that love is only conveyed in moments of sweetness and gentleness will not grow up a whole and happy person.

I feel I should explain here that my use of the word 'discipline' in this time of using politically correct language is very much deliberate. Using appropriate discipline does not mean that anybody is ill-treating children; it is quite the opposite. The word 'discipline' comes from the word disciple or the Latin word *disciplus*, which literally means 'student or learner'. I believe it is our parental duty to teach our children right from wrong, and acceptable ways of behaving and demonstrating emotion, so that they can grow to be respectful and honest adults in the community.

While the reintroduction of discipline was doing great things for Jennifer, we were beginning to find discipline totally disastrous for Robert. We really didn't know what to do for him. He was so frustrated and we felt so helpless. He desperately needed routine and discipline yet he was so sensitive that this merely left him totally and utterly desperate. The situation was pitiful. An utterance of the word 'no' or a cross tone would leave Robert screaming and thrashing. At best he would whimper in my arms for what seemed like hours. His behaviour became extremely negative and he was very difficult to direct. I wondered what had happened to my lovely little boy.

We took Robert for another hearing test. His hearing was fine, but he was referred for speech therapy and again we waited for the appointment for what seemed like an eternity. We began to pin out hopes on yet another specialist.

As the speech therapist began the initial assessment, our spirits were lifted as she reassured us that his behaviour was perfectly normal for a child with delayed speech and language comprehension and that as his speech improved so would his behaviour. Again, we were beginning to see the light at the end of the tunnel and hoped that things would start to improve soon. She suggested that if he was still having problems when he was three, he might be able to attend a language group once a week with half a dozen children with similar problems. For the first time, it was actually me who thought he would be OK by then. She offered us an appointment for three months hence and said he would be seen probably every three months. He was still not putting two words together and yet again my hope was crushed. I wondered what good could possibly be done in what averaged out at just four sessions a year.

I have to admit here that I have never been the most patient person in the world, but since having the children I have learnt more and more to try to be patient. Robert, in fact, seemed to need an abundance of patience as I found that the only way to get through the day with any amount of sanity left was simply to be so patient and calm with him that I found myself behaving completely differently to how I ever expected I would.

I tried turning a blind eye nine times out of ten and saved the discipline for when it was truly important. When it really mattered, we could then use whatever measures were appropriate for discipline at difficult times, such as if he was going to hurt himself or someone else, or if he was going to break something or run off out of the door.

Many times, I found that if my tone changed in the slightest, if my patience started swaying or my voice rose even slightly, then we might just as well wipe out the rest of the day because I wouldn't be able to do a thing with him. He simply could not cope. Some may say that I was certainly guilty of overindulgence, but we were at least getting through the day with fewer battles and traumas than previously.

Again, I have to remember that there is good in everybody and despite all this, there were still tender, loving moments when we quite simply cuddled for hours. What a wonderful way nature has of making these special children able to both give and receive overwhelming love.

We had come to nickname Robert our Lovable Rogue. It was a saying that kept us going and brought some measure of reassurance that there is both good and bad in everybody. Sometimes you have to look a little harder, but I am convinced that there is always some good. We simply learnt to look at the good in Robert and enjoy it.

10

And Then There Were Three

The following year, Jennifer started playschool and Robert went to 'Gym tots and toddlers', while I battled hard against tantrums and offending stares. I tried to pretend it didn't bother me, as I tucked him under my arm and marched home after another awkward scene. This happened whenever Robert was told to do something (or not, as the case may be), or even told it was time to go!

Deep down inside, I was embarrassed by his behaviour and hurt that even people who knew what he'd been through could still stare and say nothing. In fact, any comment would have been better than none!

Anyway, we plodded on and I got better and stronger at coping with and ignoring offending behaviour from both Robert and our onlookers. So, we could, to all intents and purposes, say that all was well. But then Jennifer's behaviour began to deteriorate into episodes of whining and whinging and generally being very irritable. I thought at first that this might have been in response to all the attention being directed towards Robert. While aware that at certain times we were unable to give both children equal love and attention, we did think that most of the time we were doing a pretty good job of sharing ourselves equally.

In desperation, I called the health visitor for advice. She came to the house immediately and reassured me that she actually did not think Jennifer's behaviour was a result of our handling of the situation, past or present. Funnily enough, though, I was more than surprised when she suggested we have Jennifer's hearing checked. I had never given it a thought, but she pointed out that after Robert's hearing problems this might not be a bad idea.

I don't know if I was more relieved or worried, as it turned out that Jennifer did indeed have a similar problem with poor hearing (although not to the extent that Robert did), and that she too in fact had enormous tonsils. So what had seemed to us like bad behaviour was simply the fact that she wasn't hearing too well and was probably in quite a lot of discomfort. It appeared that Jennifer's problems could be sorted quite easily with the same operation Robert had undergone.

The consultant's registrar saw Jennifer and described how quick and simple the operation was and how there was no need to worry. He, of course, knew nothing of the problems our son had had during the same 'simple' operation.

Of course, I worried. I went to my sister's to pick up Robert and I cried again. Part of me was relieved while part of me was desperate. 'What should I do, Jan? Do I let her have the operation or not?' I asked. Could I live with myself if I signed the consent form and something went wrong? But I knew deep down that I had made up my mind.

Jennifer was suffering and I knew the chances of anything similar happening again were very remote. I had to let her have the operation. How could I make a decision that would leave her struggling and suffering?

Two weeks after her fourth birthday, Jennifer had the procedure. I stayed with her and we were in for two days. How I cried over those two days, but I never let her see.

All went well though, I have to say, and I have never been so relieved as when they wheeled her back into the ward. I knew it was Jennifer even though I couldn't see her face. All I could see was her lovely long brown hair. I cried again as we settled her into her bed. My husband said, '*Now* what are you crying for?' Will men ever understand the emotions of women? I was crying with joy. I was so happy. I thought, 'It's all over.' Neither of them has any tonsils or adenoids now to be a problem. We can get on and enjoy life.

Jennifer was an absolute angel while we were in the hospital. She loved the attention and wasn't a bit bothered about the operation. She boasted that she was having the same operation as her brother and didn't mind taking any medicines at all. She did like her sleep though; one sedative and she was out for the count. She was quite put out that she hadn't seen the operating suite!

I was so proud of Jennifer. She behaved beautifully, and her health and happiness improved dramatically from that moment on. She was back to the old Jennifer – such an enthusiastic child and so eager to learn and please. She seemed to cope extremely well with all the changes life threw her.

Two weeks after her operation, Jennifer started school at the tender age of four years and one month (this being due to the government changes). Again, she coped brilliantly and was, of course, the most beautiful little angel of them all.

She stood in line with thirty other boys and girls, all dressed in their new uniforms. She had two long brown plaits in her hair and a beaming grin. Her pinafore was miles too long and her plimsoll bag dragged along the floor, but she looked beautiful.

While all this was going on (as if that wasn't enough), we moved house to cope with our ever-growing family. Yes, you guessed. Shortly before Jennifer's operation, we discovered that I was expecting our third child!

I think it happened around Robert's second birthday. Despite the problems of Robert's early years, we had always wanted three or four children. We loved Jennifer and Robert dearly but we couldn't decide whether or not to have another child. Should we give all our attention to our two youngsters (much needed by our son, but just how much we were still unaware) or should we have another? I loved having babies and toddlers around the house and as Robert progressed from cot to bed, it seemed he really wasn't a baby any more. I'd look at the empty cot and wonder what it would be like having just one more.

We couldn't make up our minds what to do, so we chose to do nothing. We decided to leave it to Mother Nature or the powers that be and see what happened. Bearing in mind it took seven months of trying to conceive both Jennifer and Robert, we weren't exactly expecting results for months. Of course, when you least expect it, these things have a way of happening, don't they? So after just one month of leaving it to Mother Nature, we found ourselves preparing to cope with the arrival of another baby. I must say, however, that we were delighted that the decision seemed to have been made for us. It was obviously meant to be. It had happened, and we were overjoyed.

In a way, it was probably a blessing in disguise, because had we perhaps waited a year or two or discovered the extent of Robert's problems, maybe we wouldn't have had another baby. Had we not, we would certainly have missed having Catherine in our world. She was, and still is, wonderful.

The pregnancy, the birth and Catherine's first year went so quickly. Right from the start, everything seemed to happen so fast. Presumably this was because, the third time around and already having a demanding young family to look after, you don't have much time to dwell on looking after yourself or looking to the future. We just had to get on with everything, and before we knew it, we were driving to the hospital with only twenty-nine minutes to spare before the somewhat hasty arrival of our second baby girl. This time I got my wish. My son is so special, I wanted to keep him special, and yes, deep down I still secretly wanted to have two little girls. I can't explain this, but I was ecstatic. I felt my family was perfect. Two girls and a boy; who could wish for more?

Catherine arrived in the world as she intended to carry on: in a whirlwind. Everything went so quickly. She fitted into the family perfectly. I suppose you might say, she had to. She had to learn to take her place in the family, and sometimes she may have had to wait a little longer than a first baby might for something, but she didn't seem to mind. She was always so content; she was a pleasure from the moment she arrived. We called her our Little Treasure. Maybe some of her behaviour reflected the more relaxed attitude and more confident approach of her parents. I have to say, after each child I learnt to be a little more patient and relaxed about things. You have to be, otherwise you'd be saying 'no' all the time or tearing your hair out.

Despite Robert's behaviour, we were determined, having seen how quickly the children were growing up, that we were going to enjoy every minute of Catherine's first year.

I fed her myself for longer than I did Robert. I kept thinking I'd better make the most of it, just in case she was our last. She took to breastfeeding beautifully and I enjoyed the feeling of closeness. Despite the tiredness, I fed her for about seven months and was quite sad when it came to her last feed. Catherine, however, made the decision to give up breastfeeding easier for me. She more or less decided herself that it was time to give up. As she took more bottles and more solids she became less interested in the breast, so we came to a mutual agreement and stopped. I must admit, I didn't feel half so tired, but I still missed feeding her.

Catherine did everything early; she crawled, sat and walked well before the expected age. She was into everything. We found a trail of destruction wherever she went. She wandered from room to room with a mischievous grin on her face, deciding what she could get up to next. Everybody commented on her smile and the funny faces she could pull.

I have to say Catherine had quite a character and certainly kept everybody amused. I never ceased to be amazed by the things she did; she really was a joy to have around.

Jennifer and Robert never seemed a bit put out by her arrival either. They quite simply adored her, and she likewise adored them.

As I have often said, it's a good job she came along when she did; we wouldn't be without her for the world. We wouldn't be without any of them!

11

Is Anybody Listening?

About a month after Catherine was born, Robert started playschool. He began at the new lower age of two years and nine months. It became increasingly apparent, once Robert was mixing regularly with children his own age, that all was not well. It is surprising how quickly one forgets what is expected in the normal development of young children and I had again not appreciated the differences between the progress of girls and boys. In the past few hectic months, I had also tried to put Robert's problems aside and had begun to think, as everyone kept telling me, that he would soon catch up and gradually outgrow some of his more bizarre behaviour.

It was by now, however, becoming too obvious that Robert was falling far behind the standards expected in playschool, and while one is advised not to make comparisons with other children, this is of course extremely difficult.

I had tried not to compare Robert too much to Jennifer at

his age. I found it difficult to recall exactly how she was then because she was, in fact, quite forward and I did not expect the same from a boy. Seeing Robert mixing with other boys in particular in his group, I had to admit that by now Robert was performing at a much lower level than even I had anticipated. Obviously, I knew he would be a little bit behind following his earlier traumatic years, but I was surprised to find that all of a sudden, I was reminded of the seriousness of his problems. More importantly, I realised that I should be trying to help him somehow. But how? I didn't know what to do for the best.

I decided to wait a while and see if he settled down now that he was attending playschool regularly. Things did not settle down, though, and when the playschool supervisor suggested that they could get a special needs assistant for Robert, I knew that I had to do something.

Other people, professional people, were beginning to notice that there was something not quite right. Robert had, by this time, been in playschool for a few months and his behavioural skills, social skills and language development were not improving at all. In fact, I thought Robert was getting worse by the day. The bigger he got, the more challenging he became. I knew that in our local authority the three-year development checks carried out by the health visitor were actually being done at approximately three and a half years. This was probably due to the fact that the increase in population was making it impossible for an already overstretched medical practice to test all children on time.

Having concerns about Robert's development, I approached the health visitor and asked her if she could do his development check as soon as possible. I explained that there were aspects of Robert's development that were causing us great concern so she agreed to come and assess him at home in two weeks' time.

When the health visitor came to the house, I initially felt that she thought I was wasting her time. She started to do some standard development checks and it was clear from the start that Robert was unable to complete the tasks expected of him. The health visitor suggested that we should perhaps wait a further six months and then reassess Robert. Again, I began to panic. I thought, 'No! There's something wrong with him and he needs help now, not in six months' time.'

Kindly, she carried on with the assessment and listened to my concerns. She seemed quite surprised when I explained the difficulties we were having getting through the day with so many tantrums.

As she tested him further, she became more aware of the seriousness of the problem and in fact changed her approach totally. She said then that it was a good job I had called her when I did, because as I had suspected, something was definitely not right with Robert. She suggested a few tactics to help us avoid some of the tantrums and then recommended that Robert be assessed by the clinical medical officer from the child development team.

Every morning, I watched for the post, hoping for a little brown envelope with NHS stamped on the outside. Eventually, an appointment arrived through the post and on the day Robert and I set off, not quite sure what to expect next. In fact, the doctor performed exactly the same assessment as the health visitor and by now I was actually beginning to anticipate their next move. She listened to Robert's history and gave the same practical tests that I knew he was unable to do. As expected, Robert performed rather poorly and I simply became more exhausted watching him struggle, willing him to do something. I wanted to speak to him and help with the tests, but I knew I had to watch and wait to see if he could do any for himself.

The doctor actually didn't see any of the more aggressive, wilder aspects of his behaviour but instead got the more introvert, shy and extremely negative side of him. Robert failed further in the language tests, as he refused to say a word that day. The test lasted two hours and by the end I felt totally exhausted and Robert seemed a little bit bewildered as he insisted on cuddling for hours afterwards.

As expected, the doctor explained that there was an obvious delay in Robert's development and suggested he might benefit from some extra help on a one-to-one basis. Of course, first she said he would have to be assessed by the educational psychologist. I knew by now that Robert would be asked to perform the same tasks again for somebody different and that we had more waiting and more uncertainty ahead of us. We still, as yet, had no clues as to what was wrong with Robert, if indeed there was anything wrong.

At this time my whole existence seemed to be taken up with trying to placate an extremely difficult child and maintain some degree of peace in the home. We returned home and got on with the daily battles while waiting for a further appointment. This time, the doctor came to the house. I arranged for Mike's mum to have Catherine so we would not be distracted further. This was a good move as the psychologist was with us for three hours! As expected, the tests were much the same but a little more in-depth. The psychologist listened carefully to what I had to say and was very patient with both Robert in his performance of tasks (or not, in most cases) and myself, as by now I was becoming desperate for some answers and also some solutions to our problems. She reassured me that I was not imagining things and that Robert's problems were not due to parental handling of situations. This was a great relief. However, she had to admit that she could not give us more definite answers right then but did give us some hope. She suggested that a definite period of assessment in a special nursery would be of much benefit to Robert.

The doctor made an appointment for us to see the special school with Robert to decide for ourselves if we were happy for him to attend. She left the house and this time I felt we had at least been given something definite to aim for. We were going to be able to get some help and advice and now maybe even some answers as to the cause of the problems. As always, though, my feelings were torn equally between positive and negative. I was beginning to feel that there really was something wrong with my precious son. I know I had been pressing for some time now for help and some acknowledgement of the problem, but maybe half of me was quite happy all the time there was some uncertainty. I had always known deep down that there was something wrong; it just seemed sort of final now that the professionals were agreeing and had recommended Robert for special education.

Our health visitor had been in regular contact since our first meeting and was being very supportive, merely by showing concern and phoning regularly. So, faced with the prospect of viewing the special school on my own with Robert and Catherine in tow, I didn't hesitate when she offered to come with me. A little bit of company and moral support goes a long way.

The school was lovely, and the staff certainly seemed to be dedicated to the children in their care. I saw many examples of enormous patience yet very definite discipline, obviously much needed while aiming to care for and teach children like Robert. From what I could see, there were other children with similar problems to Robert, some a little better, some a little worse. This was reassuring, as it reminded me that we weren't alone. There were other children and other parents who must be going through similar experiences to us.

I knew I had already made up my mind that Robert needed the help and we would be accepting the place offered to him, but I found it almost impossible to say it. Just to say 'yes' when asked if I'd like a place for my son seemed like such an enormous hurdle. It was probably the first hurdle in accepting fully that my son had a problem.

For the first time ever, I felt numb. I couldn't think straight, let alone talk. Every time I thought of anything I found myself crying again. For once, I prayed that the phone wouldn't ring. I didn't feel like talking to anyone as I was too emotional. Seeing all the little boys and girls in the school made me realise that Robert wasn't that much different to them. Robert really did need the help and so did we. Now, at last, it was being offered, so why couldn't I say yes?

Of course, I wrote to the school accepting Robert's place. He was to start in the January term for three full days a week.

Preparing yourself for your offspring leaving the security of home and not being entirely dependent on their parents the whole time often happens when they are about four or five years old. I felt a bit like I was losing my son to someone else's care far sooner than I should.

Why on earth are mothers so emotional? Are we doomed to feel guilty whichever decisions we make for our children? Any amount of reassurance that I was doing the right thing didn't help, either. I could reason with myself until the cows came home but I simply felt like I was sending my little boy away.

Over the next few weeks, I tried hard to be extra patient with Robert (pangs of guilt creeping in, no doubt) but found this increasingly hard. Robert was so difficult to direct in his tasks and extremely negative. Every little thing seemed to take so long and there were many tantrums.

There were eight weeks to go until Robert started in the special needs nursery, and although I knew I was going to miss him dreadfully, the eight weeks suddenly seemed like an eternity. With every day becoming more of a battle and Robert also growing much bigger and much more physical by the day, I was becoming less tolerant of the children in general and felt constantly tired and irritable. I think at one stage I lost my confidence with all the children. I didn't know what to do for the best with Jennifer or Robert and was questioning everything I did for the baby. I began to doubt my own capabilities, especially with the baby, which was silly because I found Catherine at this stage of development easier by far than the other children. After all, I'd already had two babies before her! We became like prisoners in our own home for a while, as I was embarrassed by Robert's behaviour and too ashamed even to have friends into the house. I should have been more embarrassed and ashamed that I even felt like this; it wasn't Robert's fault and we were only doing our best with him.

Apart from the necessary school run for Jennifer and playschool for Robert, we stayed indoors. By now it was even too cold to play in the garden.

Eventually, I regained my confidence and thought, so what if people stare if Robert has a tantrum? I knew he wasn't just a naughty boy; I knew he was special, so we simply had to go out there together and get on with life, get on with living. I found ways of making shopping trips and waiting in the school playground for Jennifer a little easier. Even though every outing was still pretty exhausting, at least we were out more. I used the double buggy, although Robert was much too big for this. It had the desired effect of restraining him with a reasonable amount of dignity for shopping trips. I always tried to reward a reasonably calm trip with a visit to the swings afterwards to burn up some of Robert's energy and show him that he could soon have time to play. Shopping trips or visits to friends and family had to be planned with a certain degree of military precision. Organisation was paramount to enable a reasonable trip out without provoking too much bizarre behaviour, thus leaving me wondering why I'd bothered. This went well for a while, but soon Robert was too big and heavy to push in the double buggy so we transferred to walking with reins on. Not quite so successful, but we managed.

I still felt that Robert's behaviour was getting worse by the day. Maybe it was just that some of the more physical behaviour was more obvious as he was rapidly growing. He seemed to be knocking into things more indoors and became generally clumsier. He also seemed much more disruptive and aggressive during and immediately after playschool sessions.

I can remember one particularly bad outburst of embarrassing behaviour, when we visited our local chemist one afternoon. It was just before we were due at school to pick up Jennifer. Catherine was in the buggy and Robert was on reins. Robert was touching or grabbing at everything in sight. I tried very discreetly to say a firm and definite 'no!' However, onlookers might just as well have thought I'd begun World War Three.

Robert threw himself on the floor and started to kick and scream. It was obvious he was not going to be placated. A few months earlier I would have picked him up, tucked him under my arm and marched off, buggy and all. But Robert was now much too heavy for me to do this. Added to which, in these instances he had an amazing ability to become impossibly limp! So what should I do? Drag him off and force him to walk by holding the reins close to his body, which was extremely undignified and humiliating for us both, or sit it out? Although also extremely undignified and humiliating, this was a lot less physical. Sitting it out with Robert, however, could take anything between ten minutes and an hour, both of which seemed like an eternity.

I felt far too tired to do battle anyway, so I busied myself with looking at displays, chatting to Catherine (who probably thought it all a wonderful show) and generally trying to pretend that I, or Robert, or both, were on another planet. This act of trying to be cheerful and patient is also extremely exhausting, so as soon as we reached the car I slumped, exhausted and relieved, into the driver's seat. I knew that for at least ten minutes, until we arrived at school, Robert was safe and restrained in his car seat, where he couldn't do too much harm. I tried to ignore the noise and hoped that ten minutes was sufficient time to achieve a certain degree of calm and to compose myself before arriving at school.

Another equally embarrassing and exhausting display, which on this occasion appealed to my bizarre sense of humour, occurred when we were at church for a special Mother's Day service. Robert was being generally disruptive and clumsy, and drawing attention to our pew. I'd decided that unless he was actually going to hurt someone or break something I thought it best not to intervene. Knowing Robert, this would have provoked a disastrous response, drawing even more attention to our family. So, again, I put on my silly grin, looked everywhere but at Robert and sang my heart out to the hymns. We were managing reasonably with our three children, four adult family members and another two young cousins. Not too bad, you could say. However, the bomb had to drop at some point!

The moment came in the service when we had to leave the relative safety of our pew and walk up the aisle for Holy Communion or a blessing. As Robert's recent history of behaviour had been pretty appalling, I was determined that he was going to get more than his fair share of blessing. Anything short of a miracle seemed appropriate at that precise moment, but Robert became equally determined that there was no way he was going anywhere near the vicar for a blessing. Here we go again, I thought. My brain asked, do we go or do we stay? Well, as I thought he was in desperate need of his blessing that day, there was no choice. Catherine wouldn't go with anyone but me that day and no one else was willing to be seen up the aisle with Robert, so off we went, Catherine on one arm and Robert by the collar, kicking and screaming. I think, at least I hope, the vicar saw the funny side and placed his hands on Robert's head. At the same moment, I raised my eyes upwards and whispered, 'Please give him a bigger share today.' The amazing thing was that the rest of the family said they hadn't even noticed.

Robert's behaviour was deteriorating quite noticeably, and we had about eight weeks to go before the Christmas break, after which Robert was starting at special school in January. At playschool, Robert seemed to wander aimlessly between activities. The staff couldn't be blamed, as they were not trained to deal with children like him. They could not direct him to do anything constructive or creative without provoking a scene, so they merely let him play. However, he would become more and more boisterous and come home in a high and disruptive mood.

I was explaining this point while talking to a friend on the phone. She suggested I contact the vicar's wife in a nearby parish, who ran an 'opportunities group'. The group was a much smaller playgroup catering for local children but with places for children with special needs. My friend explained that being halfway through the school term, it was highly unlikely that there would be any places available, but she suggested calling anyway, as she thought the vicar's wife might be able to provide me with advice or information.

I did contact the vicar's wife and to my astonishment she said she had a place available to start immediately. She suggested I take Robert to the group the very next week to meet her and see what we all thought. I planned for Catherine to stay with her gran, and Robert and I spent a wonderful morning together with the group. The staff were lovely. They were so softly spoken, calm and patient, yet they followed some very stringent discipline regimes. I wished I could have struck this balance. Robert's response was amazing. He was still difficult to direct and negative, but I couldn't expect too much as I was still with him and the situation was all very new. However, he was much quieter and calmer. He sat beautifully for drinks and biscuits, and played contentedly in their garden. He seemed to take very well to the vicar's wife, as did all the children, and even sat with the others in a circle for song-time, although his participation was yet underdeveloped.

Robert was much calmer at home that afternoon too, compared to his other playschool days. He had been offered the place to begin immediately; my mind was made up. I drafted a letter to his old group removing him from their register. This was quite emotional as Jennifer and Robert had both attended this particular group. My health visitor said that they did not usually advocate changing playgroups, but, in this case, they agreed it was the right decision.

The first morning I left him at the opportunity group he cried as I left, but I was reassured that it was all for my benefit and he stopped within five minutes. When I picked him up from that very first session, for the first time ever Robert came home with some craft work! He had drawn and painted just like the other children. He hadn't been given choices, you see, simply told that everybody was going to sit down to do a drawing. I was so proud! Robert's work then hung from our dining room walls as Jennifer's always had and it was lovely to see. Obviously, Robert hadn't transformed into an angel overnight, but the point I think I am trying to make is that change can occur with the right kind of help and in the right environment.

After a few sessions, Robert could walk to their garden, behaving well, holding hands; could produce craft work; could play constructively alongside other children; and if he did not join in with their singing, he would at least sit in the circle for song-time. After two months, Robert's memory was beginning to show signs of developing and he would sign recognisable snippets of nursery rhymes at home.

I will end this chapter on a light note as, despite all that had happened, I always maintain that humour and laughter are an ideal tonic.

At the playgroup, the children sang a song about a worm that goes something like this:

There's a worm at the bottom of my garden
And his name is Wiggly Woo.
He wiggles to the left. He wiggles to the right,
He wiggles all day and he wiggles all night.
There's a worm at the bottom of my garden

And his name is Wiggly Woo.

Having established that Jennifer also knew this song, we were delighted that here was a song our children could share together. There are, of course, appropriate actions to go with the rhyme. Sadly, Robert's memory was not developing as well as would be expected. Robert could only remember very limited numbers of words or activities in sequence, this presumably inhibiting his learning processes. In this instance, in particular though, one has to laugh, as Robert's version of the song, no matter how hard we tried to teach him, went something like this:

There's a worm at my bottom

And his name said Wiggy Wiggy Woo!

12

HELP

At about the same time as starting at the new playgroup, Robert also started attending a language progress group. This group was run by Robert's speech therapist, whom he was seeing at approximately three-monthly intervals. I had always thought that this was a bit inadequate, as Robert was certainly getting enough conversation and encouragement with his communication skills at home. If he was going to have speech therapy, I thought it would be much better if it were a little more frequent. This would at least enable Robert to become familiar with his speech therapist. After all, if he was to communicate at all with anybody, he needed first to build up a trusting relationship. So Robert attempted very little speech during these three-monthly sessions.

Needless to say, when the speech therapist suggested that Robert attend the progress group, I was much more optimistic and thought it would be more appropriate for Robert. I think she had to agree that his speech, in fact, was not progressing as expected.

In no time at all, Robert settled into the group and was more than happy to be left, as far as he seemed aware, simply to play with his new friends for a while. At the end of each session, the mums were invited into an adjoining room to discuss with the therapist and each other their children's progress and their performance that morning.

Robert did indeed seem to progress well in this group. When he first joined, he was still saying mostly one word on its own, whether trying to make a statement, ask for something he wanted, or answer a question. After just a few weeks, he started to put two words together like 'Daddy home' or 'juice, please'. Once Robert got the hang of this, he simply raced along, joining two, three, even four words together. It was really quite an amazing thing to watch. In just a few months, Robert became another incessant chatterbox (there's a lot of them in our family), and he seemed delighted with his new-found skill. The understanding of language and the ability to communicate are such wonderful gifts, but I'm sure most of us probably take them for granted.

Robert's time in this group, however, was short-lived. He left after only one term as he was to start at his special school and would be having regular speech therapy there. I am very grateful for the time Robert was given by the speech therapy team.

In January 1996, Robert started at Heathfield Special School in Fareham. The week before, I busied myself preparing for his first day. I made sure he had his bag ready with clean clothes (in case of accidents), and had hurriedly sewn name tags into all his clothes and anything else that would be going with him.

His first day wasn't as traumatic as I had anticipated. The first week, I took Robert to school myself. I'm sure that his past experience of changing playgroups and going to the progress group all helped to make this transition easier. I think that maybe Robert just thought this was similar to playgroup. He had no concept of time, so he probably wasn't too aware that he was staying much longer. The fact that he was given a cooked meal in the middle of the day, I'm sure, would have been a bonus, loving food as he did. The first week was probably more emotional for me than for him. The first day, he came home very excited, but also very tired. He seemed eager to return the next day, too, making the settling-in period much easier for all concerned. Robert was to attend for three days a week initially. This was quite sufficient, as he was still also to go to his playgroup once a week. We had one full day a week at home together and we very quickly made this our special day. The teachers reported that Robert was settling in well and I was reassured that again I had made the right decision. However, the second week was to prove far from easy.

As Robert had been recommended for special education, the council was to provide transport to and from school. A taxi was arranged to pick Robert up from home on the second Monday and to take him to school and bring him home each day thereafter. I had deliberately requested that I take Robert myself for the first week to help settle him in. I also thought that it would help when getting in the taxi if he knew where he was going. This second Monday was definitely going to be traumatic. An escort was also employed to sit with the children and ensure that they were safely escorted into school. Robert's escort came to the door that morning but there was no way he was going to get into the taxi without a battle. Knowing my son as I did, I simply thought it best to pick him up and strap him in his seat. This I did, then kissed him goodbye and said, 'Mummy loves you. Have a lovely day at school.' I watched, desperately, as the taxi drove away. Robert was crying and waving to me. He looked so pitiful, but I knew I had to let him go. He needed the help they could offer him. All this self-reassurance didn't stop the tears from trickling down my cheeks.

As the days went by, Robert got used to the taxi and there was no more fuss going to school in the morning. In fact, after a few weeks he seemed a lot easier to direct and a lot happier on the mornings that he was going to school. He came home very tired each day though and there would often be tears and tantrums after school. I think it is fair to say that for the first half-term (six weeks), Robert's behaviour actually took a turn for the worse. I had begun to think that things couldn't get any worse, but it was at this point that I also took a turn for the worse. I became very emotional and irritable. I was extremely low and totally exhausted, both physically and emotionally.

Robert had been at his new school for six weeks when he had his first full medical. I went to school with him that morning to be present at such an important time. I sat for a while with the school nurse and the medical officer, and we discussed Robert's history in some detail. We also talked about his present problems: the learning disability, the developmental delay, and in particular, the difficulties we were experiencing with Robert's social skills and general behaviour pattern. All of these, I was reassured, were not due to 'poor parenting', as seemed to have been the favoured statement of some doctors. After all, I had raised two very well-presented little girls, whose social graces had been remarked on frequently. Indeed, I had two compliments from professional acquaintances, both of whom said that the girls were a credit to us. What better compliment could a parent wish for? This is not to say that the girls didn't behave badly sometimes; it's just that mostly they saved the off moments for inside the safety and security of their own home.

As to the problems with Robert's behaviour, I felt greatly relieved that by now Robert was feeling more at ease in his new school and was starting to display some of his more negative behaviour in the classroom rather than saving it for home. Initially, Robert came home with glowing reports of his behaviour throughout the day. I then began to think that perhaps he was only ever going to display symptoms at home and that his teachers would think I was imagining it all. I mentioned this on one occasion and thankfully was informed that most of the children were on their best behaviour initially and only when they had settled into their surroundings and had come to know and trust their teachers would they start to show signs of 'testing' conduct.

The teachers had begun to notice some of Robert's more negative behaviour. They had also noted that, as I had always said, he found it very difficult to take adult direction, although that was improving slowly.

Following the assessment time in the early months at special school, it was suggested that Robert would probably not start at mainstream school in September as planned. I had thought his teachers would probably recommend that he stayed where he was for the moment; after all, he had all the professionals to hand and much more attention, which is certainly what he needed.

Incidentally, at the end of the assessment, Robert had to perform the same tasks as he had for the health visitor, the clinical medical officer and the educational psychologist. I had by now watched Robert do these tasks four times. I was advised that he would be expected to repeat the exercise for the paediatrician. I knew the tests off by heart and I knew what Robert's response would be. It had been documented many times by now in the written reports that had been sent to various professionals, and us, following each assessment. Maybe fifth time around Robert would surprise us all and remember the tests and perform without hesitation. Perhaps he'd score one hundred per cent!

Having said this, during the medical, for the first time, I did notice some improvement in Robert's response to the assessment tasks. It was only very slight, but nevertheless it was an improvement. People had told me that they could do wonderful things in just a short time at these schools. I must admit, though, I remained a little sceptical, especially after Robert's behaviour had deteriorated initially.

Around about this time, Catherine became poorly – in fact, on her first birthday. She had developed an infection and was rushed to hospital after suffering a febrile convulsion. Well, she had to be different, didn't she? This was something that we hadn't experienced before. I spent four days in the hospital with Catherine while the doctors tried to control her temperature and discover the source of the infection. This turned out to be a severe dose of tonsillitis.

It was during this stay in hospital that I found I had a little more time on my hands than usual (one child instead of three). I took advantage of any naps Catherine had and did the same myself. I did a lot of thinking while attending to her needs and realised that I had been quite guilty of neglecting the emotional needs of the girls. It is quite difficult while attending to the physical needs of your children and the day-to-day management of the home to remember the truly important aspects of life; to ensure that the emotional and spiritual needs of each person in the family are given sufficient consideration.

When presented with a child with special needs, it is difficult not to become so wrapped up in this one child's needs that you risk completely failing to meet the needs of the others. Perhaps I have been using the term 'special needs' too loosely; after all, are all children not special? Do they not all have special needs? I would, however, be hard pressed to find a kinder term to describe children such as Robert.

A few generations back, he would have been described by such harsh words as 'retarded' or 'backward' and he would probably have been hidden away from society. I am glad we are living now in a slightly more tolerant society. These children are now acknowledged for the amazing individuals they are and given the special assistance they deserve. We have certainly been very fortunate in that Robert had the opportunity of extra help in a wonderful school and met some extremely caring and patient people there.

During Catherine's episode in hospital, I resolved to make more of an effort to ensure that all of my children were given more quality time together as a family and individually. I decided that it was time to be much more spontaneous and natural in my approach to raising the children and to try to run a more 'normal' household. The most noticeable change had to be in my attitude to Robert. I knew that I had to stop wrapping him up in cotton wool and defending him. Instead, I had to treat him the same way as I treated the girls, especially with regard to discipline.

At about four years old, Robert reached a particularly delightful stage in his development. He became quite loving and lovable. At this stage, we were not aware that he would later be diagnosed as autistic and that this trait of showing emotion was actually quite unusual.

He was also, however, no angel; he remained extremely demanding and was prone to quite severe outbursts of temper. As most of this behaviour was due to the frustration caused by the delay Robert seemed to be experiencing interpreting the spoken word, Robert's teachers suggested backing up the spoken language with sign language. The teachers used Makaton sign language in the classroom and it had been noted that he was much calmer in the classroom and seemed to respond much more readily to visual stimulus.

I always said that we would try anything if we thought it would help Robert, so I learned the Makaton signs and tried to establish this in the home. This had an enormously positive impact on Robert's overall behaviour and improved his happiness more than I could have ever imagined.

13

The Parent and Child Game

When Robert was about five years old and still at special school, he, Mike and I attended child and family therapy at the Osborn Clinic in Fareham. Here, we were engaged in sessions of the Parent and Child Game, a wonderful approach to positive and sensitive parenting. I still use this approach today with my children, foster children and grandchildren. Positive parenting is a must for all parents. I can thoroughly recommend it and will always be grateful to that team, who will probably never know just how much they helped me throughout my children's lives.

During one session of the Parent and Child Game, Robert and I were in the playroom, which had what looked like a huge mirror on the inside of the room but was actually a one-way window. On the other side sat the team observing Robert's behaviour and our interaction. The team would give me instructions via an earpiece telling me to say positive statements to Robert and praise him for the good things he did. I was also told to ignore unwanted behaviour and not even make eye contact unless he was going to hurt himself or me.

On this occasion though, Robert had seen his dad leave the room and this time wanted Dad to play instead. He decided to try to get to Dad and spent half of the hour-long session trying to ram a push-along train through the door. I was told to look out of the window, chatting about what I could see. I talked about the cars and the trees, even about the people and what they were wearing. I was at no point allowed to look at Robert or speak to him until he came back into the room to play again. At this point I was allowed to praise Robert for coming back to play.

After the child and family therapy, on the whole Robert did seem to become calmer (although he still didn't settle until late in the evening and rose early the next day at roughly 5:30am). This bit didn't help us, as we were on the go from the moment he woke.

As Robert's speech began to improve, he became quite a little chatterbox. Conversations could be held more easily with him and he could be a delight to listen to. His speech was still difficult to understand for strangers and we sometimes forgot this, as we were used to his pronunciation and his sentence order being incorrect.

Robert was still very self-directed, making playing with his sisters quite hair-raising at times. He tended to monopolise situations and possessions, whether his or not, resulting in frequent clashes with high tempers and noise levels. Robert, however, was making progress; he was improving and learning, albeit slowly. Many people commented on the changes in Robert after he started at the special school. I still have nothing but praise and admiration for the staff concerned.

I was learning too. I learnt that I might not always get things right but that I would always try to do my best for my children, to raise them to be happy, healthy and loved.

14

Destination Diagnosis

At six years old, Robert was finally seen by a child psychiatrist and diagnosed as having moderate learning difficulties, autism and ADHD.

After struggling for such a long time, knowing that our son had quite a significant problem, the complete diagnosis was nonetheless quite a shock. We had not been as emotionally prepared for the final outcome as we had anticipated.

I have to admit that my immediate reaction and feeling was actually relief. It was simply so reassuring to know that there was a reason for our son's strange behaviour. In that moment, when we left the doctor's office, I loved Robert more than ever before because I knew that he really couldn't help the things that he did or the way he was. He looked simply adorable again, just like my baby boy.

The calmness that followed Robert's diagnosis was also reflected in his behaviour. As my acceptance of the situation resulted in a more relaxed attitude, it also became more evident that Robert and, indeed, the whole family had become much calmer.

Unfortunately, the initial feelings of relief, acceptance and calm were soon overshadowed by intense feelings of anger. I became angry at the whole world. So angry that this had happened to us, to our son. I also began to question why.

No matter how hard I tried to search for the answers, I had to admit that none were forthcoming.

It would be dishonest of me if I were not to admit that the years of struggling with a challenging child were starting to have a profound effect on those closest to Robert and their personal relationships. Although we felt that we had always accepted the situation as well as we could, we nevertheless continued to struggle with a rollercoaster of emotions.

Despite the knowledge that we were far from alone in this situation, the greatest problem for me seemed to be an intense feeling of isolation. Despite living in a house with four other people, on occasions I felt so alone and overwhelmed that at times it seemed difficult to cope. Somehow, I did; I had no choice. I somehow found the strength to carry on and did my best.

If I were to be honest now, I would have to say that the biggest problem seemed to be the relationship between me and my husband. With little support and a constantly demanding young family, exhaustion seemed to take over and left little or no time for us. The flood of emotions and seemingly endless number of problems appeared to have robbed us of any kind of normal life together.

However, for Robert, at six years old, life was good. His hyperactivity and learning difficulties were his main problem, but he was unaware that he was different to anybody else. He had not questioned why he went to a different school, and until such time as he did we remained happy that, in this instance, the age-old saying of 'ignorance is bliss' certainly remained true. That is not to say that Robert was or is ignorant; far from it. Underneath, it was obvious that there was a wealth of intelligence and an amazing personality waiting to be unlocked.

Around about this time, a house move to be nearer to family and friends who could offer support was suggested. This turned out to be a particularly distressing move, as my husband refused to come with me. My mood was very low at the time, so against all my better judgement I proceeded to move myself and the children to live with my family, in my original home town of Waterlooville.

After a few months, my husband joined us and we decided to buy a larger, older house in Purbrook. We thought that the extra space would be great for the children, but the house needed completely refurbishing.

I think the shabby surroundings in which we were living were the penultimate catalyst in provoking my mental illness. The final straw came when our younger daughter, Catherine, needed the same operation her brother and sister had undergone before her.

I was already pretty ill when Catherine was admitted for her operation at three years old. I managed to hold it all together while she was in the hospital. However, just one week after her surgery, I was admitted to St James' Hospital in Portsmouth because I was unable to care for myself, let alone my children. This was the start of a particularly distressing time, as I was to spend a large part of the next two years in this hospital.

During my first admission to this hospital, Jennifer took her first Holy Communion in our family church. I was given home leave to be with her at this very special Mass and at the party afterwards. Although I was there in body, which was so important for Jennifer, I knew that I wasn't there in mind. The memory of this event remains a bit of a blur. I do, however, have the most beautiful photos to remind me of the day and everyone was so pleased to see me there.

Another very important event when the children were young, which I missed, was Robert's transfer to mainstream school. At this time, I had been admitted to the Marchwood Priory Hospital in Southampton. A shortage of NHS emergency psychiatric beds resulted in a stay at this private hospital.

I cried all that day. I should have been there on this very important day for Robert. I cried and cried as I told the nurse that I had let my boy down so badly. It was a day he really needed his mum and I wasn't there!

Robert's transfer from the infants to the mainstream school actually went very smoothly. Robert's first year in senior school was also relatively uneventful. He seemed to settle quite well, but he was never really very happy. He didn't smile as much and he certainly didn't laugh much any more. I had anticipated a certain amount of regression with this transition, as this often occurred for Robert at times of significant change. I never really thought he would cope with school life in a mainstream secondary school. Even though the school had a special needs team, I knew that it would be an extremely challenging period in Robert's life.

The thing that stands out in my memory most at this time is that Robert started to have seizures. When he came around from these episodes he would be unresponsive and very floppy. On two of the occasions, Robert went blue around the lips and paramedics were required, as he needed oxygen therapy. An

ECG revealed that these seizures were not epilepsy; however, they were extremely alarming to watch.

We eventually learnt to cope with these new events in our lives, and to adapt. Eventually, the frequency of the seizures decreased and they finally stopped altogether a few years later.

Robert became quite negative, difficult to direct, obstinate and often verbally abusive, as he was about to encounter the most difficult time so far in his life – namely, adolescence!

Adolescence can be a thoroughly distressing time for many teenagers, but for Robert it really knocked him completely off balance. As a young teen, Robert was at his most difficult, even more so than as a frustrated toddler with no speech. He demanded more patience, tolerance and support than ever before. Once again, I was accused of overindulging him by well-meaning family and friends. I found this especially upsetting, as I too needed patience and support.

Despite being a teen, Robert would still seek comfort in a hug from me. I will hug Robert until the end of my days if that's how he needs reassuring. As Robert navigated the teenage years, I felt, more than ever, that we had to demonstrate to him that he was very much loved and a worthwhile person.

For much of his adolescence, Robert withdrew from family and friends. He would seek solace and comfort in the sanctuary of his bedroom and on his Xbox, where I think he felt safe.

Luckily, a new programme to support students with special educational needs was being introduced and this helped Robert enormously, even boosting his very low self-esteem. Robert was offered a one-day-a-week college course to run alongside his mainstream education. He was able to choose a practical course, which they hoped might enable him to achieve a more suitable qualification. Robert chose to study catering during this course and was welcomed wholeheartedly by Chef Paul and his team at South Downs College.

Chef Paul and Robert shared a wonderful relationship built on mutual respect and understanding. Chef Paul helped to lift Robert's mood and he gained much confidence in this setting, with adults supporting him who were both fully accepting and dedicated to ensuring equal opportunity and inclusion. In this setting, Robert thrived.

Robert was an extremely brave young man throughout his education. Despite the difficulties, he managed to cope with the mainstream school system and also paved the way for others who followed in this new era of inclusion.

Quite remarkably, despite poor predictions, Robert even coped well with attempting GCSE exams. He attended every exam he was entered for and wrote well, with his special assistance package. He even travelled home alone (never before attempted), as I was, by then, physically very poorly. He remained happy and positive, and I believe he deserves a medal for all this, even just for trying.

I like to think that if nothing else, I have taught my children to love themselves and accept themselves as worthwhile, unique and lovable people. As they go through life, they, in turn, should radiate love, laughter and compassion to all with whom they have contact.

Incidentally, Robert excelled himself in his GCSEs. He achieved far better grades than the teachers and computers predicted. He was predicted all F and E grades, but managed to come away with three grade Es, two grade Ds and a fantastic grade C in probably one of the most difficult, controversial, thought-provoking and sincere of all subjects: religious education. Many employers believe a qualification in this subject shows great strength of character and I agree!

Alongside Robert's wonderful sense of humour, with which he entertains and inspires me continuously, he also seemed to have acquired great strength of character and determination! Robert went on to train as a chef at college and worked reliably and conscientiously for six years as a valued member of the local Asda team. He is an inspiration!

Because of Robert, I decided to remain determined to champion the profession of full-time devoted motherhood and to ensure that it is recognised as the worthwhile, significant and vital role in society that it is.

15

Bitter Pills

Exactly one week after Catherine's operation when she was three years old, I was admitted for the first time to a psychiatric hospital. This was to be one of many long stays I was to endure during the next two years.

The doctor diagnosed postnatal depression with severe obsessive-compulsive disorder. I was distraught because I had to leave the children for some considerable length of time, but I couldn't look after myself, let alone the children. I believed wholeheartedly that this hospital and its drugs were going to make me better.

At one stage though, I realised that I was taking a cocktail of seven psychiatric drugs. I seem to recall trying such drugs as clomipramine, Clopixol, temazepam, Prozac, Piriton, olanzapine, diazepam, procyclidine, Stelazine, clonazepam, Flurox, lithium, sertraline, amitriptyline and thioridazine. Not that I took all of these medicines together, but there were various combinations used in an attempt to make me better. And these are the drugs I can remember. There were many, many more.

What the next two years had in store for us seems hard to believe. I was so very, very ill and recalling this time made it a difficult and emotional subject to write about.

I don't necessarily recall many individual side effects of the drugs I was prescribed, but seem to remember an overall cumulative effect, which meant that I was always trembling and shaking and had this awful feeling of being completely detached from my own body. In fact, not just my own body, but life itself and all those around me!

For most of those two years, I felt as though I was a ghost. The best way I can describe that 'ghost-like' feeling is if you watch Patrick Swayze in the film *Ghost* when his character (a ghost) tries to move a material object as he would have in life, but is unable to do so. It is phenomenal and also extremely terrifying!

Even more terrifying than that feeling, is that now, with hindsight, I realise that on several occasions while I was in hospital, the drugs made me practically comatose, and I, completely unaware, was unable to move or respond. On two separate occasions this happened in an alarming manner.

On the first occasion, without any recollection or awareness of what was happening, I was dressed, and sat in an armchair where I remained slumped for the rest of the day. I didn't eat or drink, and neither did I move or respond to anything or anyone. At that point the worst thing happened; unfortunately, my husband brought the children to visit. I was totally unaware that they were there. I didn't respond to them and showed no signs of recognition. How on earth this was allowed to happen,

I will never know. Imagine how frightened my children must have been.

There is no point in feeling anger now, or attempting to apportion blame, but surely, at the very least, there should have been better communication between those responsible for my care at that time and my family. There was, in fact, a complete lack of communication! Surely the doctors and nurses could have warned my husband about how ill I was and asked him not to bring the children to visit that day. Their visit should have been rescheduled. They should never have been allowed to see their mother in such a state!

Years later, when I learnt of these events, I tried to put myself in the mind of a child and imagine how they might have felt. What if they hated me for being like that? What if they thought I didn't love them, as I didn't respond to them? This haunted me for some time as I thought how, from a child's viewpoint, it may have seemed. They were only three, five and seven at the time.

I often wonder, when I think of that time, if the doctors and nurses really believed they were helping me. I was so very ill. I don't believe that it was very good practice at all.

At that time, I was so ill, I couldn't communicate to anybody how I was feeling. That's when I realised that I had to start fighting to make sure that this never ever happened again. Not to me, to the children or anybody else. This is also probably why I felt I needed to write my story: to try to prevent it from ever happening again, and to prove to others who might be experiencing similar health problems that you can beat it but that it is not necessarily always the doctors or their 'wonder drugs' that are needed.

With the right support I think anybody can beat it, but *you* need to want that and *you* have to be strong. I was determined that I was never going back to that awful place again, but it took a great amount of strength for me to get well. And I was determined that I was never going to be parted from my children again!

However, there was worse yet to come, one more severe event to follow, and I am only glad that on this occasion the children weren't present to witness it.

16

ECT and Me

The worse to come was in fact the several awful occasions I was given ECT, electroconvulsive therapy.

Unfortunately, I actually gave consent for this treatment myself. However, at the time, I was not in my right mind. Just as I was not in my own mind when I attempted to take my own life. My personality had been completely changed by the so-called 'wonder drugs' that were supposed to be treatment for the better. The side effects of these drugs were catastrophic. I was not 'me' any more. I could not think clearly nor could I make a sensible decision. With hindsight, I think wholeheartedly that I should not have been asked for my permission for such barbaric treatment, as I did not possess the mental capacity to be making sensible, or even safe decisions about my life. At that point I would probably have agreed to anything.

Later in life, while training to become a foster parent, I learnt that ECT should never have been prescribed or allowed to go ahead, and I should not have been asked to make my own decisions in agreeing to go ahead with the treatment. I find it hard to believe that this practice was still being used in the year 2000, and it is even more disturbing to know it's still in use today. This is very dangerous territory, and something I feel we are not addressing well enough in British society.

Having said this, while actually experiencing ECT I did, in fact, feel some benefit – only in the very short term and only while actually under anaesthetic for the purpose of the ECT itself though. When sedated with anaesthesia I actually felt so relaxed, almost in a trance or even death-like state, the deepest form of sleep one could ever imagine. This is the only way I can describe the feeling. Surprisingly, I felt 'recharged', which is a weird choice of wording when you think about what they were actually doing to me, but it truly made me feel like I had slept for years. I was reinvigorated! Shockingly, I began to look forward to the ECT sessions. Thankfully, it wasn't long before the doctors finally realised that this was not a very safe, kind or even humane thing to be doing to me.

There was also a further horrific event. I had become so comatose with the side effects of so many medications that I did not get out of my bed. I did not eat, drink or even go to the bathroom for three days. I woke from this awful situation on another hospital bed where I was being held down and was being forcibly catheterised. This was not a humane way to be 'caring' for the mentally ill members of our community. I was scared and felt violated, terrified and angry all at once. This is when I finally vowed that I would find a way to get better on my own and that I would most definitely not be coming back to this hospital.

Incredibly, one understanding nurse at the hospital realised that I was not in the right place to receive the treatment I needed. My OCD was a very complicated form and they were not experienced enough to help me. Somehow, she managed to get me referred to the most wonderful hospital I have ever been fortunate enough to visit.

I was referred to the Maudsley Hospital in London where there were doctors and therapists specialising in severe forms of OCD. Even better news was to follow. To be admitted to this hospital you had to be medication-free. I was, therefore, gradually weaned off all those awful medications and became physically much better very rapidly. I knew nothing of the Maudsley and its methods, but I knew that there were thousands of people like me waiting to get appointments, so I embraced the opportunity and went in with a very open mind. I saw this as my 'last-chance saloon' and had already decided that I would give 110% to all that was asked of me. I knew it meant a further three months away from the children as an inpatient in London, but I had already been so ill for so long and had missed so much time with them. This was a small price to pay for the 'happier, rest of our lives together' outcome that I so wanted. I knew this would be a short-term pain for a much longer-term gain!

I was finally admitted to the Maudsley Hospital on 14 February 2000. This was my 'new millennium'! My husband and I ate lunch as a Valentine's Day treat in the hospital café before he left me in their hands for what was to be my biggest and best experience in the field of mental health care.

17

The Maudsley

I don't know how, or why, Chris helped me so much at the Maudsley but she did. She was one of those truly amazing people and I took to her right from our very first meeting. Chris was allocated as my personal therapist on arrival at the Maudsley. She would be working with me, I was reminded, every single day during my stay.

I was admitted to the hospital and shared a hostel-type ward on the perimeter of the hospital grounds with eight other OCDers. We were a mix of people: male, female, young adults, older adults, heterosexual and the odd gay person. It was actually really lovely.

We each had our own bedroom and then shared bathrooms, living room and dining room. There was a small two-bedroom flat attached for those who were progressing but needed to practice independent living. This had a kitchenette, lounge, bathroom and two bedrooms.

I loved my bedroom at the Maudsley. I can still recall it now. My bed had a plain blue duvet cover and then I had a set of drawers and a desk. It was reasonably large and was my home for the next twelve weeks. I actually only stayed ten weeks in the end as I did so well that I didn't need to stay the length of time of most people.

Initially, our day was to involve twice-daily sessions, dropping down to daily sessions in the hospital building with our therapists. We were also assigned homework sessions, which were mostly of a practical nature. In the future, we were going to be allowed home visits, when it was decided we would be able to cope.

I was seriously ill when I came to this hospital. I could hardly touch anything for such a deep-seated fear that something bad would happen and then I would pass this to others. I was literally a nervous wreck. My first meeting with Chris, though, gave me a great deal of hope. We got on really well and when she left the room for a minute I took a sneaky look at what she had written about me on the computer screen. What I saw lifted my spirits. It read, 'I was delighted to meet Joanne, a lovely, kind, warm, 34-year-old lady.' I didn't read any further. I was just so happy. She hadn't seen any bad in me despite what I'd told her about my OCD symptoms and my past. What she saw was very different. She saw an illness but more importantly she saw a 'person', and not a bad person either. She also saw that my illness was just like any other illness that needed the right treatment in order to heal. She mostly saw a 'lovely' person and that person was me.

I began to realise how low my own self-esteem was, how little I thought of myself and how I always thought I must be a bad person! I also started to think a little differently though.

I began to wonder if maybe I'd been wrong all this time. If this lady, whom I had just met, could recognise good things in me then perhaps I was not so bad after all. But it then began to dawn on me that the message that I was a bad, unworthy person had come from the person who should have loved me the most, the person who should have loved and protected me, keeping me safe no matter what. I began to feel sad as I realised that I had been wronged for many years by the very person I trusted and loved, as any person would: my own mother.

The treatment I was to be given was CBT, cognitive behavioural therapy. This treatment was relatively new then, but is widely used and accepted now. I was going to be taught new ways of thinking about things, and new ways to respond to things. I was excited and I wanted to do well, for Chris, because she was so lovely, and first and foremost, at last, for myself because I felt I deserved to live a better way. My children deserved to have their mum at home with them and, more importantly, stay at home with them and be able to touch them and care for them as she wanted.

I was also relieved, because I only had to take one of the many previous drugs I had taken, and this remaining one had few side effects. The best thing was that I had no more ECT!

That first session was mostly about getting to know me; however, Chris did set my first piece of homework right away.

That evening, knowing how much anxiety I experienced when touching anything brightly coloured, Chris had asked me to sit at the dining table in the hostel, take an orange from the fruit bowl and hold it in both hands until I could stand it no longer. She also knew that after this I would feel compelled (remember earlier I explained about ruminating and compulsions) to go and wash my hands immediately. She knew

I would not be able to touch anything else until I had done this, but she wanted me to wait as long as I could before washing. She also wanted me to take note and describe to her later what I was feeling throughout this task.

I sat at the table with my hands in my lap, holding the orange. Knowing that we were all dealing with unusual habits and had equally unusual homework tasks, none of us patients ever asked each other what the other was doing! It was like an unspoken rule – you just didn't go there. Everybody there was so respectful of each other. We were all suffering in a similar, yet unique way.

As I held my orange, I could feel the anxiety rising in my body. I knew this feeling; it was part of me. However, usually when I could tolerate it no longer, I would act. I felt the panic rising higher through my body, my legs, trunk, arms, heart and finally towards my head. My hands were trembling. I had never allowed the anxiety to be taken to such a pitch before. I now know that Chris wanted to prove to me that what I feared would happen never actually would. At that point, I felt that my whole body was literally about to explode through my head. Don't ask why – we sometimes don't figure it all out. I did say OCD is completely irrational and that's why it's so terrifying. Anyway, I would normally have given in to my compulsion long before it got this far. But, as I continued to hold on to my orange, instead of actually exploding at the highest point of the anxiety, what happened instead was that my stress began to reduce. This was phenomenal for me. I had achieved so much in just one piece of work. I'd gone past the point of no return, but nothing had actually happened.

Sitting there, my heart rate slowed down again, my breathing slowed and quietened, and the panic subsided. I think

I may have actually cried, too, at that moment. I still felt the compulsion to go and wash my hands, but I didn't rush to the sink. I wanted to bask in my triumph a little longer. The next day, I was able to describe all these little details to Chris. I don't think she expected such a remarkable breakthrough so quickly herself either. I was quite shocked too. Pleasantly though.

Another equally notable piece of work I did with Chris, we actually worked through together. Chris wanted me to go into the art room, knowing how much colour and dirt terrified me, and sit at the work bench and paint a picture. I thought she was joking to be honest. She wasn't! She came with me to the art room though, guided me in and held my hand as the terror wrapped its ugly arms around me once more. I was ashamed too. Ashamed because I couldn't control this awful feeling that took over at the most random, strangest of times. Despite this, I sat down and I even took a paint brush. I pushed my brain and the awful feelings it threw at my body beyond all the limits that I thought I could never ever face, let alone conquer. Now, I'm no artist, but I painted a stick-person picture of my family. Believe it or not, once the blanket of terror started to slip away again, amazingly, this began to feel quite good. I discovered that art work was extremely therapeutic.

In a few short days, I'd already learnt so much about my own brain and body and I'd also learnt to enjoy new things. That evening, I joined other patients at the hospital chapel for their version of *Songs of Praise*. It was just a group of about ten regulars, all patients with different mental health conditions. One was a young lad, maybe about eighteen, who could hardly function in many areas of life, but boy could he play the organ. Not only that, but he could play whatever hymn we requested, and he could do so totally without music. He was amazing. The patients came from all the different types of hostel dotted around the outskirts of the main hospital. There were us OCDers, a hostel for those with eating disorders, one for mothers and babies, and another for hoarders and so on. Nobody judged anybody else. It was lovely, just to be able to be yourself, warts and all, and no one minded.

At the 'Songs of Praise', we were each allowed to choose one hymn that the young lad would play and we could sing, or not if we didn't want to. To be perfectly honest, I was so moved during these evenings, and emotional after my achievements, that I spent the first few sessions just crying. But that was OK – no one minded. I made lots of new friends here too. Once I could join in and actually sing the hymns, I repeatedly asked for the same hymn: 'Father, I place into your hands'. I offered up my troubles to God and he helped me. I was so grateful for that time in the little chapel at the Maudsley. This also sparked my desire to reignite and deepen my relationship with Christ and the church when I returned home. In the years that followed, this proved to be another institution that would help to raise my self-esteem and become a source of my healing, comfort, support and love.

There were several opportunities for socialising at the hospital. One of my favourites was karaoke night. My friends and I would use the little community hall and have a bit of a sing-song. I had never before encountered so many different forms of OCD or of anxiety. This was an eye-opener for me and taught me much about compassion and empathy. I will never stop being grateful that I had the opportunity to go to this hospital, especially considering the enormous waiting lists. I feel very privileged and blessed to have had this opportunity.

I never met my consultant, but his name was Professor Marks, author of *Living with Fear* and many other books written to help those suffering from anxiety. It's a great book and his methods at the hospital certainly helped me. I still use CBT to this day.

Chris knew that I liked to read and to write short stories, so with this in mind, she set me another piece of homework. She asked me to write a description of any one of the paintings hanging on the walls of the hostel. I enjoyed this homework, and wrote about the most colourful picture I could find. That was when I realised just how much I truly enjoyed writing too.

Our next big change was that after two weeks of being an in-patient, all of us were expected to try a home visit. As my home was some distance away from the hospital and I had never travelled independently on public transport, it was decided by my team that my family would visit me at the hospital instead. We were to be allowed to stay in the flat for the weekend and the staff planned for extra beds to be put in for the children. To be honest, I was nervous about them visiting. Maybe I was becoming a little institutionalised. I worried about how they would respond to this environment and the other patients. I wondered if they felt that I'd abandoned them. I didn't know if they understood that I wasn't well. So many thoughts were rushing through my head.

Friday afternoon came around and Mike drove the children to see me in London. I was excited too, despite the nerves, but mostly worried about how they would react when they saw me. I need not have worried at all because the next minute I saw all three of my children running up the path to the front door. They practically threw themselves into my arms, hugging me and telling me how much they loved me and had missed me. We had a lovely weekend. We went into the shopping areas, ate lunch out, played lots of board games and watched TV; it was just perfect.

Catherine was only five at the time and she fell in love with one of the young male patients. She asked him to join her in playing Monopoly. I thought that he might feel pressured, possibly raising his anxiety level, but he played, over and over again. The innocence of children. I think, in some way, she may have helped him.

At the four-week marker, however, it was expected that I would travel home to spend the weekend with my family. Added to this, it was expected that each patient would make his or her own way to their home, no matter what distance, on public transport. Although my lack of experience in travelling independently on public transport had been the reason for my family visiting me previously, this time there was no way out. I had to make the effort, but I found the whole idea terrifying.

Chris printed out the route for me and even included bus and train numbers and timetables. I had to take the bus to Victoria train station, then a train, followed by a coach back to Waterlooville. I was also terrified in busy, crowded places. What if I took the wrong train or missed the coach? I trembled each and every step of that first journey home. But I did it! I was so proud of myself. I made the same trip each weekend thereafter until I was discharged home. I think this travelling really helped to give me back much of the confidence I had lost over the years. I never imagined that in the future I would be able to travel alone to Spain, drive long distances and enjoy travelling to new countries!

There was much more that occurred at the Maudsley but these are the things I remember the most. Suffice to say, I did so well that I was discharged home after ten weeks instead of the usual twelve weeks that is expected of patients at this hospital. The time at the Maudsley helped me learn so much about life, myself, my feelings, emotions and relationships, and about the importance of enjoying life. I am glad to have had the chance to go to this hospital and will never regret the time spent there. This was one of my best life opportunities and time well spent in a fantastically caring and compassionate environment.

18

Revelations

It was February 2007 when I tried to leave my husband, Mike, for the third time. I'd previously tried to leave him when we moved back to the Waterlooville area in 1998, when I first became ill with OCD.

The second time I left him, or asked him to leave, we were apart for two weeks. He begged me to take him back, telling me he couldn't understand why I'd even want to be apart. He felt that he had never done anything wrong and that there were no problems in the relationship. Still, he offered to compromise on lots of things that bothered me except for the one thing that I wanted more than anything: another child. The children wanted their daddy home and I decided that the happiness of the three children I already had was more important than what I wanted. So I took him back with his promises to make compromises in his behaviour towards me and the children. These promises, generally, only ever lasted for two days.

On this third time we separated, again I asked him to leave the family home, which was our lovely bungalow in Silverdale Drive. This was our supposed dream home. I had wanted the move here in 2004 to be a special new beginning for the family, with me now at my optimum health both physically and mentally, or so I thought. I'd hoped to provide a kind of fairy-tale ending, a happy-ever-after scenario in the children's lives in this lovely new home. I wanted it to be always full of happiness, with no bad times.

Having a dream home and being more comfortable, however, is like the old adage 'money doesn't buy happiness'. Having a nice big house to live in is never going to make a person happy if they're not happy with the people they are sharing it with.

At the same time as this move, I'd also been trying to wean off the psychiatric drugs I'd been prescribed years back. With the help of my fantastic GP, I was able to gradually stop taking a drug called thioridazine and eventually also another medication, called clomipramine. These were the two medications I'd stabilised on with the fewest side effects for me. I'd tried several times to withdraw from these drugs because they made me feel so awful and I wanted my own brain back! I wanted *me* back, not somebody else in my body!

Previously, I'd tried many times, unsuccessfully, to come off these medications. In retrospect, I realise the pattern that was emerging every time I attempted this, but at the time it was hard to see clearly. When I was 'off' the drugs, I began to think more clearly and realised that I didn't like the way I was living, or the way I was being treated.

It wasn't the houses or the children, but the way I was being treated by Mike, who was causing so much pain. I don't think

Mike is too academic or even very clever at all; however, he was smart enough to think that if I got a bit low, or started suggesting things like separation, all he had to do was march me back to the doctors and have me put back on psychiatric drugs, and the problem would go away.

In a way, he was right. But this was a very simplistic way of seeing the situation. I'd begun to realise that these drugs only dampened my spirit and masked the symptoms, without ever actually addressing the real problems or helping to resolve things and allow me to be truly healed. Seeing it like this, I also realised that the drugs just made me submissive enough to tolerate an intolerable situation. All this while Mike was sharing with friends and family that he was 'caring' for his sick wife and three children. He actually never stepped in to help me with the care of our children, or myself, unless I was deemed sick enough to be in a hospital. No matter how poorly I was, if I was home I was expected to take care of everything: myself, the children and our home. I soon worked out that Mike would only ever believe somebody to be poorly if they were sick enough to be in a hospital bed!

So here we are, at the third and penultimate time that I attempted to separate from Mike. After asking him to leave the family home, I finally confided in most of my family, although at this point, I wasn't ready to tell my father or the children. I told the rest of the family that maybe I shouldn't have entered into the marriage at all, as we had too many pre-existing issues. These issues concerned honesty, loyalty and trust. Pretty important aspects within a marriage wouldn't you think?

I had got to the point where I wanted Mike to show me in his actions, not just with words, that he was willing to make the same amount of commitment to our marriage as I had when

I married him, in the presence of God, and despite the knowledge I had. At that time, I also thought I was strong enough to be able to cope with all this. For a while I was, but one person can only handle so much.

The main commitment I wanted from Mike was for us to try for another child. Despite already having three children, the difficulties we'd had with Robert and pressure from others to forget the idea, I still felt overwhelmingly maternal. For once, I also wanted to say, 'To hell with what others want, this is my life.'

I seemed to have spent my entire life trying to please others. In my youth, I had tried to please my parents, falling short every time in the eyes of my mother. This was followed by a twenty-year marriage trying to please both Mike and children. Now I wanted the choice to do what I wanted before it was too late. Also, I was very much aware that my female biological clock was fast running out of time.

When I mentioned wanting another child, Mike went absolutely 'ape shit'! He stormed out of the house shouting that I needed medicating. I felt that I was just a woman wanting to do exactly what nature intended for women. I couldn't control my maternal feelings. If that's a sin, then I stand correctly accused. However, I certainly didn't think it was fair for others to stand in judgement, be critical and condemn me for this. Had I not been so busy trying to please everyone else, I may have had a fourth child earlier!

I had come so far in my battle to keep the OCD at bay and going through the withdrawal of long-term medication that I knew I had the strength not to give up easily this time. I was clear in my mind for the first time in ten years and I was *not* going back.

After Mike left, the children were extremely distressed and Robert (fourteen) and Catherine (eleven) hugged me for hours. Jennifer (sixteen) went very quiet; she doesn't share emotion so readily as some in our family. I'm afraid I wear my heart on my sleeve. I cry in Mass; I cry when I listen to moving music; I cry when I'm happy or sad. In fact, I cry for many reasons, though not always through sadness.

I needed some emotional support, so my best friend and my auntie came to visit, because Mum, whom you would expect me to turn to, had left for Spain when Catherine was six.

During this separation, I spent two weeks alone with the children. I began to feel quite calm and we managed pretty well too. Robert and Catherine still kept asking when Daddy was coming home. This time, Jennifer had stopped asking. I agreed to meet Mike, as he asked, for a chat in the nearby pub. We never went to a pub usually. Yet again, he managed to transfer all the blame for our situation onto me. He could see no fault on his part whatsoever. He made me feel like I was being unreasonable, especially when he added, 'After all I've done caring for you!'

I was, by now, however, beginning to work out the difference between 'care' and 'control'. I'm not sure if he did this with intention or if this just came naturally to him, but I was suddenly shocked at the realisation that there had never been any care, there had only ever been control. I recognised I'd never had any say in our home situation: how money was spent, where we would live, or where we would go on holiday. I even had to account to him for every single penny that I ever spent. And I do mean this literally. Mike was always self-employed and was very strict with how money was spent, looking back now, possibly to the point of obsession. He gave me a small allowance each week, which had to cover food. He organised payment of all household bills and even decided how the child benefit should be allocated. If I wanted clothes or anything else for the children or myself then I had to ask his permission to purchase such items. He would only give me permission if he agreed it was a necessity. He made me feel guilty if I spent any money on myself. Occasionally, if I was feeling very angry or rebellious I'd go for a bit of retail therapy, a spending spree. Once I lived as a single parent in reality, I did become a bit of a shopaholic for a while. Money burnt a hole in my pocket. I liked to spend. This was a new-found freedom and I did get a bit carried away sometimes, simply because I could. For the first time, I didn't have to ask anyone's permission. I learnt to be more sensible though, as I knew there was only me to provide for everybody.

During the meeting with Mike in the pub, he once again made me feel ungrateful. I felt bad for the children too, so as we chatted we both agreed, once again, to make compromises. I forgave him, again, and he returned home. The only thing he would not compromise on was what he called 'the baby problem'. He made it a condition of his return that I was to forget this 'silly idea' and never mention the word 'baby' again.

I knew that the only other option would be for me to leave Mike for good and take a chance on finding a new partner this late in life who would be prepared to have a child with me. To me, though, this seemed a ridiculous idea. I felt strongly, and still do, about the sanctity of marriage and the family. I had taken my marriage vows extremely seriously. I so wanted and intended for it to be till death us do part. So I took him back.

I was also still thinking of the happiness of the three children I was already lucky enough to have. Adding a new partner and possible half siblings was, for me, out of the question.

I was devastated that this event had marred the plan I'd had for this home to be our happy-ever-after scenario. But I tried, once again, to make things work, to be a good wife and mother.

Ironically, just eighteen months later I needed an emergency hysterectomy! All my hopes of ever having another child were to be finally removed, once and for all, and there was nothing I could do. I was only forty-two when I had my hysterectomy and many would say that I was already too old to have another child, but where there's life there's hope, so to speak. Now, I knew there would be no hope, ever!

At this time, I seriously thought about turning away from my faith. It seemed that all things bad were happening, but what actually occurred was the opposite. These events only deepened my desire to become closer to God. I felt it was 'Him' who kept me going when all else was going wrong, especially when, for the fourth and final time, just four months after my surgery, I separated from Mike and prepared properly for life as a single parent.

One of the strange things is, when I confided in my family GP that I was going to leave Mike, and knowing that he knew my entire medical and family history, and also shared the Catholic faith, he actually surprised me with his response. He had become very supportive following my hysterectomy and my suspected Sjögren's syndrome, and had also been very involved in caring for my son over the years. He once said to me that despite how much pain he knew me to be experiencing, both physically and emotionally, he never saw me cry unless I was speaking about my love and devotion for my son. He said he admired my bravery and shared that he felt I had this amazing inner strength I was able to draw on when I needed it most. But he also noted that my feelings of protection and devotion for my son were my Achilles heel.

This particular doctor had also seen me with Mike while we were still married. He had once suggested to Mike, while I was recovering from the hysterectomy, that if he noticed my mood was ever getting low again, he was to take me back to see the doctor. By this time, I was becoming much stronger emotionally and much more confident in myself as a person. I had also come to know my mind and body very well indeed, much better than most people do. Therefore, on this occasion, I spoke up. I said to my GP that if *I* noticed that I was feeling low, then *I* would make the decision to come back to see him. I told him that I knew myself the best. I think this is when he first realised just how strong I was and how much more confidence I had in my own self.

When I made the decision that I could no longer remain in such an unhealthy marriage I went along to see my GP. I knew that it would be a difficult time for me, given my past mental health illness. I told him I was going to leave Mike and his response absolutely astounded me. He said, 'I actually commend you for what you're doing.'

He continued to say that he felt it took an enormous amount of courage, given that others would possibly judge me to have lost my mind, but he had witnessed the controlling nature of the relationship with Mike and said that he would support me wholeheartedly. Also, being a Catholic himself, he knew that I was very strongly loyal to my faith and it was this that had prevented me from leaving sooner. He said that he believed that on this occasion my faith had maybe held me back, adding that God would not want me to be so unhappy that it affected my health.

What he also told me was to prepare myself for a great deal of emotional abuse and blackmail to come. He shared his admiration for my strength of faith and when I shared how guilty I felt, and that I didn't deserve to be teaching others in our church community, he surprised me even further. He said he couldn't think of a better person to be representing our Catholic community in this manner. I don't think I've ever had as many compliments in my life before.

It's funny, who and what situations help give you back your confidence and make you feel more positive about yourself, after a lifetime of low self-esteem. When people such as my counsellor at the Maudsley, many of the doctors caring for me in the various hospital departments and wards, and even members of the clergy recognised me as a good person, only then did I finally start to truly believe in myself.

At last, you begin to realise that you are deserving of good things after all. My middle adult years were a big turning point for me. A time of positivity and healing.

I had wanted Mike and I to grow old together, to be a Darby and Joan couple. As I've mentioned, I took my marriage vows extremely seriously and expected us to stay together until death. I grieved for my marriage for quite some years after this all happened. Our time apart during separation, for me, hadn't meant that our marriage was completely over. There was still hope, but I needed time apart to heal from all the hurt, and I had already told Mike what I expected from him if he was serious about our marriage.

While professing his undying love, in words, during the separation time, he was, however, still putting other things above me and his family. The marriage could then not be reconciled, as he decided to meet, and move in with, another woman while still legally married to me. I was then, and always have been, completely loyal and faithful to my marriage vows. He had no grounds to divorce me and, although completely against the idea of divorce myself, I had no option but to file for such in order to protect myself and the children, to be free to recover and start providing fully for my family.

I separated our finances completely, got a job and even put our house up for sale. I moved myself and the children to a smaller terraced house within walking distance of my church.

Earlier in this chapter, I mentioned pre-existing issues around honesty, loyalty and trust. So what was the terrible secret I had managed to keep quiet for all of these years?

Seventeen years earlier, on the evening that Mike and I were to announce our engagement, my mother told me that she and my fiancé had been engaged in a relationship of a sexual nature! Mum sat down quietly and calmly to make her announcement. She explained that while she and Mike had travelled to Andorra (the place where I had first met him), with a view to jointly purchasing a holiday chalet as a business venture, they had, somehow, managed to end up sleeping together, in the fullest sense of the word!

I was devastated. It felt like my heart was broken into millions of tiny pieces. I was also indescribably angry. You name it, I probably felt it and my language at that moment reflected that. It was extremely colourful! (I didn't yet have OCD.)

Why ever didn't they tell me earlier? If they had owned up to their sexual liaison earlier in our relationship, when I was not so strongly in love with Mike, I may have been more able to walk away. As it was, I thought I loved this man with all my heart and, having been brought up as a good Catholic girl, I decided I must forgive them both. I did, and then made a huge

114

commitment to both relationships by remaining friends with my mother and marrying Mike, despite everything they had done.

My mother had had previous affairs, some of which she openly shared with others, including family members and even me and my sister. Despite this, she was still claiming, years later, to be married to our father. But what makes this worse is that if my mother hadn't thought that I should know this and that I could cope with such things, this may well have remained a secret that Mike appeared to happily bring with him into our marriage! I don't believe he would ever have shared this. Sometimes I wonder if I would have been better not knowing. Who knows?

But good old Mum! We were brought up to always be honest and Mum also felt that we should be strong, independent people like her. She believed we should be able to cope with all that life throws at us. It would be many years before I was able to accept that she actually thrived on drama and attention. I have yet to work out why she had become such a power-hungry, assertive, aggressive, angry and bitter person.

It also took many more years for me to realise that both my now ex-husband and my mother were very controlling, almost abusive people. I think they now call these relationships 'toxic' relationships. I can see why.

As you can imagine, moving forward from all of this, including how she had abandoned me as a teenager, impacted on my own mental health, and my relationship with her and Mike during our marriage.

When my friend and auntie had come around to support me emotionally during one of our separations, I shared the secret I'd been holding in my heart for the last seventeen years.

Everything spilled out like a tidal wave; it all came crashing onto the shore. I must admit I felt an enormous sense of relief that I no longer had to carry this secret. It was like a massive weight lifted off my shoulders. Years of carrying that burden had taken its toll on both my mental and physical health.

Having never mentioned my secret to anyone, I suddenly felt really awful. I'd just related a nasty story about my mother, sharing it with her sister. However, she knew my mum so well; she'd grown up with her. My auntie even has counselling herself to be able to cope with her relationship with my mum and my grandmother, who was also a very domineering woman. This auntie is one of the strongest, loveliest and kindest ladies you would wish to meet.

Then, of course, Catholic guilt kicking in, I felt I needed to apologise. I said, 'This is the truth, you know. I couldn't and wouldn't make up something so awful.'

There is a lovely saying that goes, 'No matter how small or humble a home, it is greater than the biggest palace when blessed by God'.

My home was blessed by my priest and my friend, Father Kevin. It then felt like my own lovely little palace. Somewhere for me and my children to call home and somewhere to be safe, and, at last, I was safe.

Now I had control, no psychiatric drugs making me feel unlike myself, and no one controlling anything for me. Just me and the children.

Once settled in our little house, my mind was still always full, worrying about getting things done and about the children, especially Robert. But by then there were noticeably many more times when my mind was quiet and calm. The children accepted that there was no other way. I had been both mentally and physically so unwell within the marriage. They understood much more by this time and were very supportive of all that followed. During the final years that Mike and I were together, with the children being so much older, I think they saw enough to realise that the relationship could not be sustained. It was not a healthy way to live. I think they saw that he did, indeed, treat me much like a second-class citizen, at times, even like a servant, and they understood that this was no way to treat a spouse. I just wanted us all to be happy in our little piece of heaven on earth.

19

St. Dominic's Priory

After my surgery, and before the next of many more, I went to stay with the Dominican Sisters of St Joseph at St Dominic's Priory in the New Forest. I went for a retreat, some much-needed rest, TLC and to spend time deepening my relationship with Jesus. While there, I spent a lot of my time at Mass or in prayer. I prayed the rosary with the sisters and with the friends I made at the priory. I spoke a great deal with Sister Julie, sharing my troubles and searching for answers. My friend Geraldine reminded me that God had come to save the sinners not the righteous, as I had shared with her that perhaps I really was a bad person. She told me she didn't believe that to be the case. She said, 'You are not a bad person. You are here, in a convent, searching for your answers with God. I don't think that is how a bad person would deal with all this.' Pointing to the lovely, newly built chapel in the grounds of the priory, she said, 'In there is where you'll find your answers.'

After I'd shared how much guilt I felt about my marriage ending, another friend from my home parish said, 'Show me a God who would want you to be unhappy all of your life.'

I received so much support from my priest and my fellow parishioners, I began to feel I really wasn't such a bad person after all. I felt good to be truthful. Where I once felt that I didn't deserve to be in church, in God's house, I now began to feel most comfortable there, above all other places. Church was 'Home'.

While at the priory, I finally realised that Jesus was my best friend. He always had been; it just took me a long time to work it all out. I had to giggle to myself as I thought about how I could share Him with everybody when I returned home. However, I thought that if *I* told people that Jesus was my best friend and could be theirs too if they let him, they'd probably think I was plain loopy! But then I thought, 'Well, they already think I'm loopy, so, hey, isn't it better to be loopy with Jesus at my side than just plain loopy?'

In all seriousness, I did wonder how *I* could do God's work and teach people about Jesus.

I didn't have to search long to find the answer to this question. I was asked to teach the children in the parish in preparation for their first Holy Communion. I happily agreed, but what was even more remarkable for me was my very own sister and best friend was teaching alongside me. I also taught the adults preparing to convert to Catholicism through the Journey in Faith programme, sang in the folk choir and attended parish council meetings as a member of the committee. As much as I gave to the church, I received so much more in return. God's love is all powerful. None of us are perfect, but we can try to be good Christian people and be kind and considerate to each other. At the time, I believed I had much more to give, but I wasn't sure yet how that would pan out. I decided to put my trust in God.

At the time Mum said, 'You don't have to do all that at church to make amends you know.' Maybe I'm too sensitive and read too much into what people say, but it felt like she still thought I was bad and needed to make amends. I was beginning to learn to speak up for myself and not take everything that people said to me without explaining my point of view. I didn't feel I needed to make amends to anyone, and I told her as much!

I do try to explain things diplomatically and sensitively though, as I don't like confrontation nor would I want to offend or upset anyone, intentionally or otherwise.

I'm reminded here that Jesus came to save the sinners, the lowly, not the righteous. I involved myself in church activities because I enjoyed it. It's that simple. I loved the children I taught and I still love teaching adults today. I get so much pleasure from these ministries, I wish I could do more. It is in giving that we receive! I have received so much in friendship and love from what I have given and it's magical. I love giving.

Parish life helped me to put the pieces of my life back together again, slowly but surely. But the limitations with my now constantly failing physical health made it difficult to keep going sometimes, as pain engulfed my entire body through every waking moment.

20

Dad Passing

Dad's health began to fail a year after my hysterectomy. In January 2010 he was diagnosed with bowel cancer and lymphoma.

It was a Friday evening when Dad was rushed to hospital. Jan and I had been popping in most days anyway over the last few weeks, just to spend time with him, and make sure he was OK and had everything he needed. But most of all to break the tension that always came along whenever Mum stayed with anyone for more than a couple of days. Mum had returned from Spain to 'visit'. As it was a Friday, we had invited her to our usual Friday girlie night at mine, but Dad wasn't well enough to be left alone so we decided to hold our Friday night at Dad's place instead. As we parked and walked up his drive, Mum came rushing out of the front door in her usual panicky mode for anything out of the ordinary, shouting, 'The ambulance is coming!' In her panicking gibberish, she tried to explain.

It seemed that Dad had suffered a rectal bleed that made her something akin to hysterical. To be fair, Jan and I were used to all sorts of medical emergencies with our nursing backgrounds, but it didn't really help Dad with Mum overdramatising every event.

We went inside, where Dad was still sat on the toilet. Mum had flushed it, so we weren't able to establish if it was as bad as she was saying. Actually, Dad was prone to haemorrhoids anyway and these can lead to quite a bit of bleeding in themselves. As Mum always overexaggerates and is very dramatic, it was hard to know, and we never will know if this situation was urgent enough to warrant an emergency admission. Especially as Dad already had such advanced cancer and had expressed his desire to stay in his own home.

I was pretty poorly at the time and caring for my own family alone, and Jan was working more or less full time, but we would have found a way to make sure Dad was properly looked after. And when the time came, we certainly wouldn't have left him alone with Mum. She was never any good with illness anyway. She always made out that she would help and told all her friends how she had looked after her 'sick' daughter in the past, and her grandchildren. Now she was telling all and sundry that she had returned from Spain to nurse her sick 'husband'. Funnily enough though, it hadn't suited her to be married to him for the last twenty-eight years. In all honesty, with her lack of patience and her aggressive temper, the novelty of looking after anyone always wore off very quickly, and she would soon be continually angrily and loudly complaining about them.

She always managed to make the situation about her too. 'You don't know how hard it is for me', she would say, or 'You have no idea what I've been through', and worse still, 'You don't know what he's put me through'. As if she were the only person in the world who ever had any problems!

We were all struggling to cope, but Jan and I would have managed fine if she hadn't returned, and would have taken it in turns to sleep over. We were already visiting daily. The Macmillan team would have supported us too. As it was, I wondered deep down if it was Mum's way of passing over the responsibility. But I had wanted Dad to be where he wished. Of course, I didn't want him to die at all! I didn't want any of this to be happening, but we all knew that it was inevitable. However, when the time came, I wanted Dad to pass away quietly in his own bed with the people he loved most around him.

In the weeks before he was admitted to the hospital, I was lucky enough to have had some lovely quiet moments at home with him. Mum needed lots of breaks, and Dad did too, and I wasn't working at the time, for which I am so grateful.

One such afternoon, Mum went out to get some shopping and prescriptions. It was always best to let her do the jobs that required a trip out and offer to sit with Dad rather than do those jobs because it gave them both the break from each other that they needed. I would much rather have spent the time with Dad anyway. I was always glad of these moments, as it was lovely to have him to myself. Sometimes we'd sit and chat quietly, other times he'd sleep, and as I was poorly too, I'd be quite happy to have a little rest myself, but always keeping one eye on Dad. This particular afternoon, I laid down on the sofa to rest, but didn't dare sleep. I kept my eyes on Dad, as he, sitting up in his arm chair, slipped in and out of sleep. His arm would drop down by his side, and Ginnie, Mum's dog, who was lying at his side, keeping guard, would lick his hand, as if to say, 'It's OK. I'm here for you!'

On another lovely afternoon when I had Dad all to myself, Mum was out for a long time and Dad was resting in his bed, again drifting in and out of sleep. I lay on the bed beside him and we chatted occasionally when he woke. This time, I just rested my eyes when he slept. But not my ears. I listened for any movement or changes in his breathing that might suggest he was getting worse or was in pain. As Dad slept and I rested my eyes, it started to rain and it was lovely listening to the rain beating against the window, knowing that we were cosy, warm and dry indoors. Then it started to thunder, and lightning strikes lit the sky. The thunder woke Dad, and, just like when I was a little girl, he started to explain, very quietly, that if you counted the number of seconds after the lightning strike until the thunder clap, you could tell how many miles away the storm was. It made me smile as I remembered. With the next lightning strike, we started to count together, still quietly. We got to five. 'The storm is five miles away,' he said. We counted again and again, each time the lightning struck. The timings started to increase. 'Ah,' he said, 'the storm's moving away now.' It was just such a lovely conversation and then, as it turned colder, I covered myself over, sharing his duvet, and we laid quiet and still for a couple of hours as the storm moved further and further away. I wanted to stay like that forever, holding that moment and never letting it go.

On that Friday, as we waited for the ambulance, Jan found some clean pyjama bottoms for Dad and helped him into them and I made Mum sit down and try to calm down. The ambulance crew were lovely and I wanted to travel with him in the ambulance. Stubborn as always, Dad insisted that he was fine and that we should stay with Mum to help her to lock up the house, get him a few bits together, and, above all, to try to keep her calm. He probably thought that she'd forget to lock the house properly as she was in such a flap. As they shut the ambulance doors, he just waved and said, 'I'll see you there.' I think he just wanted a bit of peace for a few minutes to be honest. He probably knew he wouldn't get any for a while.

When we arrived in casualty, Dad was actually sitting up on the trolley and looked quite good. I was pleasantly surprised. But it was a Friday evening. We waited and waited for the doctors to see him and when they did they couldn't find his notes and knew nothing about his cancer diagnosis. They didn't seem to know what to do for him. There hadn't been any more signs of bleeding, but the doctors decided to admit him anyway so that the oncology team could see him and decide what to do next.

They transferred Dad to the Medical Assessment Unit and tried to get him comfortable for the night. I didn't want to leave his side, not even for a moment, but he was stable enough, so we kissed him goodnight and promised to return in the morning. I didn't sleep much that night and wondered what on earth the next day would bring. I just kept thinking, 'We have to get him back home! He wants to be at home!'

Saturday morning, I was up early and got myself bathed so I knew I was clean and could spend as long as possible with Dad. I phoned Jan and Mum to arrange lifts and Jan phoned Dad's sister, Midge, to say she'd pick her up to take her to the hospital. Mum and I went together and, again, when we arrived Dad looked surprisingly good, if a little grey, but he had looked a bit grey for the last few months.

The ward was really busy but Dad was tucked away in the corner so we pulled the curtains half across and made ourselves comfy around him on the chairs. We weren't going to leave him, so we knew we might as well make ourselves at home. We knew it would take a long time, in a hospital on a Saturday, to get anything done or any decisions made, if at all.

We found a newspaper and started to do the crossword between us. Quite funny really as I'd never been any good at spelling, Scrabble or crossword-type games. I have a big sense of humour and I needed to use it to lighten the mood and the sense of desperation we were all secretly feeling. I wanted to make Dad laugh too, to see his lovely big smile. We fooled around a bit and kept ourselves and Dad entertained. At last I actually managed to answer a question and fill in one of the words and Jan said something about, 'Where did that come from?' I had a bit of a rebellious reputation at school and played hooky quite a bit so I jokingly replied, 'That must have been one day I actually went to school. I remember learning that in a lesson!' Mum and Dad, though strict, knew that I had been somewhat troublesome and this did, indeed, bring a smile to Dad's face. When I actually managed to find a second word, it was Dad who exclaimed, 'Oh my, that's two days you went to school!' Everybody round the bed roared with laughter, including Dad who seemed thrilled that his joke had pleased us all. We continued in this vein, taking the mickey out of each other and telling tales of mischievous antics of the past until I really had to get up to go and spend a penny – all the laughter no doubt. In truth I didn't want to leave Dad's side, not for a second, but needs must.

As I rounded the corner of the ward, my Auntie Chrissie was coming towards me. She asked how Dad was and I dissolved into floods of tears! I didn't, and wouldn't, show my sadness in front of Dad, but inside I was terrified. I was terrified of losing him. Next to my children, he was my whole world. He'd always been there for me and was our biggest support. I couldn't begin to imagine life without him, I didn't want to, but I had an idea he was pretty sick by now and there was nothing I could do to control this situation. Chrissie was wonderful, as always, but as I didn't want Dad to notice any redness in my eyes, I sat in the waiting area with my Uncle Graham for a while and had a cuppa and a hug.

The oncology (cancer) doctors weren't sure whether or not to give Dad a further course of chemotherapy, so they took a load of blood samples to see just how much or, indeed, if any benefit had been achieved with the previous courses. In the meantime, as Dad was immune-compromised due to all the chemo, he was moved to a single room with en-suite bathroom to protect him from the risk of infection from other patients. He was moved into this room on the Sunday and it was much nicer for all of us. It was quite a big room so we could all sit with him quite comfortably. We spread out a bit and I have to admit, we even used his bathroom ourselves so that we didn't have to leave him for long.

I can't quite remember why, but they took Dad for another couple of radiotherapy sessions. But the news wasn't good when the blood results came back. Dad had gotten worse; his results were pretty devastating, even to his doctors, and there was no more they could do for him other than keep him pain-free and comfortable. I managed to hold it together for a while to talk to the doctors. Mum asked how long they thought he had and I was alarmed to hear them say, 'About a week, maybe a bit longer.' He had still been pottering about a little bit at home before he was admitted. Then, when I thought about it, I realised that he hadn't even been able to lift his legs up off the mattress since he'd been in the hospital. I wanted to make sure though that I communicated

Dad's wish to be at home very clearly to the doctors. They agreed that if that was his wish, we would all work together as quickly as possible to achieve that goal.

Mum was the one who, after the doctors spoke to Dad, spelled it out clearly to him. I wondered whether that was really necessary. He knew, and he understood what the doctors were saying. Yet again, I thought, she was being overdramatic for her own benefit, not for anyone else's.

While she was speaking to Dad, I spoke to his nurses, who were very fond of him and were equally shocked. One nurse in particular had become his favourite and she always tried to find custard for him as he had very little appetite but fancied custard. I tried to tell her a little bit about the person he was. When I went back in to the room, Mum stepped outside and I just said to Dad, 'Do you still want to be at home?'

He nodded, so I said to him, 'Then will you let us look after you properly with the help of the Macmillan nurses?'

He nodded again and I think I said then, 'You do know I love you, don't you Dad, very much?'

I'm sure, and hope, but don't remember if I actually said this to him, or just thought it. Dad wasn't one for showing his emotions. He was a very proud man, and he would hate to let anyone see him cry. I didn't want to make him cry or cause him either pain or embarrassment, but I needed him to know how much I loved him. Even though I said it to him most days of my life. But I am pretty certain I did say it, because he answered, 'And I love you very much too.'

I didn't mention it again quite so specifically, and as I found myself alone with him again, I just didn't know what more to say. What can you say, after such devastating news, to such a proud and private man? I just said, 'D'ya fancy a hug?'

He was obviously very emotional, and couldn't speak, but I was delighted as he opened his arms and we hugged like I was his little girl again! Jan was at work and we still had to tell her all this latest news. She is extremely sensitive and emotional, and as Mum and I stepped outside, to discuss how to tell her, I did then sob, uncontrollable, heavy sobbing. I couldn't hold back, and I was shaking badly. I kept saying, 'This is so much emotion, I can't bear it. I actually feel like my heart is going to explode.'

And that is exactly how I felt in that moment. After all the conversations and explanations, after all the practicalities, I gave in to the realisation of what lay before us, and I honestly believed that I couldn't cope and my heart was going to actually explode with all this emotion.

While arrangements were being made for Dad to come home, or so I believed, Dad was moved again because he was no longer an assessment case and the bed on that ward was needed. Dad was moved upstairs to the oncology ward. He now had to share a room again with four others, but he did have a lovely big bed area in the corner by a huge window, which made it quite bright and warm.

Yet again, we made ourselves comfortable around his bed. We had been staying at Dad's bedside all day, every day, since he had been admitted. By the time they actually managed to move Dad's bed though, we had had to leave, as it was about 11pm. This was the Tuesday evening. It was also Holy Week and I should have been at church every day with the candidates who were being brought into the Catholic community at the Easter Vigil, the Saturday before Easter Sunday. The whole of Holy Week was booked up for me, but I couldn't and wouldn't leave my dad. I made my apologies and arrangements for a substitute, and I hoped that they, and 'Him Upstairs', would understand.

On the Wednesday, we still hadn't managed to get Dad's arrangements made for transfer home and he became much worse. The doctors prescribed diamorphine for his pain and I knew now that we weren't going to get him home. We asked one more time, 'Dad, do you still want to go home?'

But I think maybe he was getting scared by now because this time he said, 'No, I think it will be safer if I stay here.' I was heartbroken, but it was his decision and I guessed that maybe this was all pretty scary and he probably did feel safer with the doctors and nurses close at hand. But I also wondered if it was more because he knew that Mum couldn't cope if he was at home and I'm certain he knew she didn't want him home. Somehow I think she forgot that it wasn't actually her home, and never had been. It was his home. But the decision, for whatever reason, was made, and it was Dad's decision, so we obeyed.

On the Wednesday night, we didn't go home. Dad was drifting in and out of consciousness and there was no way I wasn't going to be right there by his side. We had gone home late in the afternoon, but the nurses phoned in the evening, as we had asked them to, to say he was worse. I think Jan must have gone from work and she had brought Midge. She knew I would drive like a mad thing because I needed to be with him so she got my brother-in-law to drive me. I kept praying all the way. 'Please don't let it be too late. Please don't let him die alone. Don't let him die without anybody with him to help take away his fears. I want to hold his hand and let him know I'm there and let him feel how loved he is.'

We all arrived together and Dad was still there. I pulled my armchair as close as I could by his side and snuggled up to him so he could feel that I was close to him. I smoothed his head, held his hand and laid my head very gently on his shoulder. He seemed quite settled, so every now and then I sat back a bit and tried to sleep on the chair. Jan did the same on the other side. Midge couldn't stay like that all night and went home to bed but Mum actually slept really well, across the bottom of Dad's bed. I know she was sleeping soundly because she was snoring loudly.

The children sent text messages saying to tell Grandad how much they loved him. It was heartbreaking watching Dad and reading those texts. Of course, I told him lots of times then how much we all loved him, but he was pretty much unconscious all the time. I don't even know if he heard. They say the hearing is the last sense to go, so I hope he heard.

Thursday morning came and we had to leave his bedside to get something to eat and drink to keep our strength up. Mum had started making sarcastic comments about our behaviour or things we said, particularly to me, and it was actually getting very hurtful. I couldn't believe that now, under these circumstances, she was being her old aggressive, harsh self. At one stage I had to walk away for fear of saying something harsh myself. It wasn't the time or place for family rows or arguments, yet it seemed that she was deliberately trying to provoke one. I couldn't believe it. She actually started to look at me the way she does when she is cross with anyone, with pure hate in her eyes. She actually scares me when she's like that. It's especially hurtful when your own mother looks at you like that. I wonder if she knows she looks at people, even her own daughters, like that. Now, several years down the line, I think there must be some kind of extreme psychological problem because of the way she behaves. It's not right. It's frightening.

On the Thursday, having been told by the nurses that Dad could go on like this for days, maybe even weeks, I went home for a bath and a sleep. We had agreed that we could not possibly sleep at the hospital like this for days on end. After my bath, I ate a little and had then slept. I woke at 11pm but something told me that Dad wasn't going to go on for days on end and I dearly wanted to be with him at the end of his earthly life.

I went back to the hospital and settled beside Dad in the armchair. He was restless and his body was agitated. The nurses gave him more diamorphine and I held his hand, reassuring him with my words that I was there and would not leave him. He settled and I curled up again gently against his shoulder. Dad was still with us in the morning, but his breathing had changed so the nurses advised me to call the family back.

Jan, Midge and Mum returned. We kept vigil all day. At 2:30pm, the nurses moved Dad to a private room. On the way to the room, my sister told me many years later that she joked with Dad, even though he was unconscious, saying that he was going to the penthouse suite. As Dad's bed was settled in the new room, I held his hand and thought that he gave a big smile. I commented on this. The nurse then got out her stethoscope and quietly checked his chest. I knew, by her whole demeanour, that this was nearly time. Later she would tell us that as one passes from this life, the last expulsion of air can cause the face muscles to move. So as I sensed something was wrong by the nurse's quick but quiet movements, I cried out, 'Please Dad, no, not yet, not like this!' I had wanted to get him comfortable and sit with him a little longer in private. Midge, too, said something like, 'Don't you bloody dare go now!'

But Dad had passed quietly and peacefully, I think, from this world. Mum fainted, if I remember right, thereby gaining herself much attention from the nurse. But I also remember wondering why she wasn't crying, because Jan, Midge and

I sobbed. I sat on the edge of his bed, stroking his face and still telling him how much I loved him. It seemed like hours passed. I didn't want to walk away and leave him alone like that but there was no more we could do. My thoughts turned to my children and how I was going to tell them this, although deep down I guessed that they would know, at least Catherine and Robert would, as soon as I returned home. (Jennifer was studying archaeology in Jordan.) I sensed that they knew I would not leave the hospital now until he had passed, as I was determined he would not be alone or afraid and had told them this. I was right. Despite not wanting to go, the time came to say our goodbyes and leave Dad. As I walked into my lounge, Catherine looked up at me with pitiful, pleading eyes. I guessed she wanted me to say everything was OK, it was all a big mistake and Grandad was all better. I couldn't tell her that though and my heart broke all over again as I just nodded and whispered, 'I'm so sorry, Grandad's gone.' Catherine, Robert and I sobbed and hugged for what seemed like an eternity.

Dad passed away on Good Friday, 2 April 2010 at 2:50pm. Such a gentle, caring man and such a good man, who with no religious following was still the most Christian person you would ever wish to meet. And he had passed away on 'God's Friday' (the true and original name of Good Friday in the past before the word 'God' became corrupted in the English language to 'good') at a similar time to Jesus himself. I truly believe that this was God's way of assuring me that my earthly father was, indeed, a very good man.

21

Following Dad's Passing

After Dad passed away, my sister and I began the daunting task of arranging his funeral. As his next of kin, this fell to us and we wanted to make sure he had a send-off to be proud of. But even darker times were about to cloud our days. Already very poorly, but as yet unaware that I would soon be diagnosed with Sjögren's syndrome, I was feeling very weak and had been for approximately two years by this time. My body was racked with pain each and every day. Despite this, we pulled together to read Dad's wishes and made sure that everything was perfect and as he wanted for his funeral.

However, as we sat in the office at the funeral site of Dad's choosing, our mother sat in an office of a very different type. She sat in a solicitor's office instructing legal representatives to act against me and my sister over our father's estate. Dad had worked his entire life to ensure that he could help relieve the burden of life's financial pressures on me and my sister. He and my mother had been separated for the last twenty-eight years, during which time my mother had even lived in another country. She had stated to others that she never divorced him due to religious reasons.

Mum hadn't wanted to be his wife in any sense of the word for those last twenty-eight years, as far as I could tell, so I question the morality of this, as well as the legality of contesting his legally written will, which stated that his estate was simply to be shared equally between me and my sister, his only living heirs. Death is said to bring out the best or the worst in people. Thankfully, it brought out the best in me and my sister. I wish I could say the same about others.

Imagine our horror, when, in the midst of our grief, just a few days after our father's death, we were served with legal papers stating that our own mother was acting against us and we were required to respond. While we should have been concentrating on our own grief and that of our own families, we were also having to seek legal advice and sit in solicitors' offices. Often in tears, we instructed our solicitor, who was equally shocked by the situation, to 'deal with this and our mother in a dignified, compassionate and respectful manner'.

Many of my friends felt that what our mother was doing was an outrage and it provoked several strong and angry responses. Due to both my sister and I having the loving and forgiving nature of Catholicism, we were able to listen to and accept the advice of our wonderful solicitors. This was the firm Dad had chosen to act on his behalf throughout his lifetime, and they continued to act on his behalf after his death, in an appropriate manner, as opposed to the angry, aggressive nature of the correspondence from our mother's solicitor. Our solicitor even commented that we must have inherited our kind, compassionate and respectable nature from our father.

Needless to say, this became a long, drawn-out battle, which caused a further rift in our already fragile relationship with our mother. It was at this time that I truly began to realise the full nature and impact of the destructive nature of Mum's relationships. I began to realise that I had always felt uncomfortable, continually criticised and consistently thinking that it was all my fault, and now finally I knew that the problem did not lie with me.

I realised that she would never change, that I would never please her and that she would never be the mother we so hoped for and wanted so badly. We didn't want anything extra special, just a mother like most of our friends had. A mother is supposed to love you and make you feel good, not make you feel bad and unwanted or unloved.

Thankfully, along with the realisation and acceptance also came a time of healing. For me anyway. I fear for my sister, as she still doesn't talk about emotional or difficult issues. Over the years, I've come to realise that actually talking about these difficulties and seeking help and support is the better way. I have had many counsellors over the years and when you find one with whom you gel then it can make a world of difference to your future outcomes.

Dad had left his home to me and my sister, but Mum was living there, against his wishes. This meant we could not visit the house to grieve in the loving, familiar environment as we wished to. Some ten months later though, Mum disappeared off the face of the earth, apparently leaving her solicitors unpaid and out of pocket.

Finally, we were able to visit Dad's house and put his affairs in order. However, this was still a very emotional time. As we prepared to sell this beautiful family home that held so many loving and comfortable memories, it became clear that I, for one, was not yet ready to part with this important place in our lives. I bought out my sister's half; she was delighted by the decision because the home remained in our family possession where we were all still able to enjoy its loving feeling, wrapping its arms around us on a daily basis.

I was worried about telling the children I wanted to move into Dad's house, their grandad's. I thought they might think it was weird or feel uncomfortable about it. So I asked them about it while we were camping and not distracted by mobile phones and technology. Dad had actually lived in the same road as us anyway, just fifteen doors up, and when I shared my thoughts with my now adult children, quietly, in the peaceful countryside not far from Dad's resting place, I was pleasantly surprised by their response. They all shouted excitedly and immediately wanted to share with their friends saying, 'Yeah, we're going back to Silverdale Drive. We're going back where we belong! Happy days.'

Yet again, my mother disappeared from my life. I didn't know where she'd gone but discovered later, from an auntie, that she'd travelled to Cornwall, the place her parents were from, and was renting a cottage. I felt more comfortable knowing there was some distance between us and she couldn't or wouldn't be able to just pop in or turn up unexpectedly. It was to be another year before I heard from her again.

The day Mum made contact again was interesting to say the least. At the time, I was physically quite ill with a diagnosis of an autoimmune disorder called Sjögren's syndrome and was having further repair surgery following my hysterectomy. I still had pockets of endometriosis surrounding my bowel. I had just been to the hospital for a really horrible, degrading investigation, and was resting up and being thoroughly spoilt by a good friend. I received a text from 'Mum' simply saying, 'Do you want to join me for Sunday lunch?'

I feel really bad looking back now, but my first reaction was to shout to my friend, 'But I don't have a mother!' I guess in order to block everything out, after Dad passing away too, I reinvented myself as an orphan. Strange, really, as I was forty-three then. But I truly felt that I no longer had any parents, as there certainly weren't any nearby, or supporting me. When it dawned on me that this really was my mother making contact, I just asked, 'What shall I do?'

Most of my friends know my whole history. I never keep anything back and I share everything. I wear my heart on my sleeve and I speak openly and honestly with anyone who will listen. There are no skeletons in my closet. My friend simply said, 'Tell her where to go', or words to that effect. She has a much braver, more assertive personality than I. Well, I didn't tell Mum where to go. I was brought up to be a decent and moral person and I was also very much enjoying being back in the fold of the Catholic community and do believe wholeheartedly in forgiveness, but I was a bit older and wiser by then. I was also learning to become more assertive and speak up for myself, so I agreed to meet with Mum but knew that I had to talk about difficult issues and especially about what had gone on in order to begin to move forward with any kind of relationship.

I knew that I was going to make it clear that, while I may have forgiven her, I had not forgotten all that had transpired and all past issues. But most importantly, if there was to be any hope of a mother and daughter relationship, it had to be on my terms and at my pace. I was too ill to be dealing with drama and I was concerned that if I got my hopes up for a change in my mum and the way she treated people, I was likely to be hurt again. There was already a pattern emerging. We'd get sucked back into a relationship with Mum (my sister, my auntie and I) only to be hurt and abandoned again at a later date. I was much too tired of all this to keep revisiting it.

22

A Very Natural Burial

Dad left us instructions that he was to be buried in an eco-friendly coffin, wearing naturally degrading clothing, at a beautiful spot he had chosen at the Natural Burial Site in a woodland setting on the South Downs. It truly is a beautiful spot! His words when explaining why he had chosen this were simply, 'It looks like a very nice place to rest.' He wasn't wrong.

Dad was quite often right on many matters. I have since purchased my own final resting place, right next to Dad at this very beautiful place. I will be lying beside my father when my time comes and the whole family often sit on 'my spot' already when we visit Dad's grave and chat together. We visit even though he said we shouldn't, because we will never stop loving him, never forget him and take comfort in sharing things with him. His body may have left this world, but I believe his spirit, his soul, whatever you want to call it, remains watching over us, especially in places close to him and to us.

Dad's funeral was never going to be easy – tell me one that is – but we were determined, my sister and I, along with our children, to make this a beautiful and fitting celebration of, and for, our dad. He had specifically shared that there was to be nothing religious about his funeral; he didn't believe in any of this despite being a truly decent and respectable gentleman. He did, however, love music and we had some very special pieces in mind, with very personal memories for each of us, that we decided to play at the graveside. We played the 'Grand March' from *Aida*, one of Dad's favourites. He loved band music and I had been involved with playing the trumpet all through school. He supported every event I played at and loved classical music and opera from a very young age too. So, music choices were easy. He had also stated no other ceremony with vicars, priests or others speaking about him.

It was decided, and rightly so, that I would write our father's eulogy, his life story and tribute, and that I would also read this. I had read at other family events previously and had spoken at church meetings and on other official occasions, but never had I spoken at such an emotional time before. I wanted to do this though. I wanted to share all the good things about my dad with everybody. I wanted to sing his praises from the rooftops! My children, at this time still only 15, 17 and 19, also wanted to read and speak about their granddad. My elder daughter was stuck in Jordan on an archaeological expedition and couldn't fly home due to an erupting volcano in Iceland spreading ash in the airways. She was heartbroken not to be able to join us. She was doing exactly what my father would have wanted though – travelling and seeing the world. But my son, despite his autism, wanted to read a poem for his granddad and my younger daughter, like me, wrote and read her own beautiful tribute to my father.

The coffin was to travel through the woodland walk to the burial site on a cart pulled by an old, black, shire horse, aptly named Sam, which seemed rather a coincidence as Dad had owned a black dog with the same name as a young man, when he lived and worked in Africa. These were all beautiful, appropriate things that should be a part of Dad's life celebration. Things he loved and things we would all know and remember about him.

The first difficulty on the day arose because the funeral parlour would be bringing Dad in his coffin to leave from his home. This was the home now belonging to my sister and me, but where our mother still resided, and we could not gain access. So as we arrived at Dad's house for his final journey, we were greeted by our mother in the drive instructing us to use the back gate and enter through the back door of the conservatory. Even on this day, she made a point of letting us know that she had changed the locks to the front door so as to prevent us entering our lovely father's home. Our home!

So many emotions were expressed that day but despite the awful things that were also going on behind the scenes, I did not want anger to be a part of the day. This day was about Dad, and celebrating his life. He was a good and gentle man who would not want us to be fighting or feeling anger. The thing is, though, we may have been able to control our own feelings, but we cannot control the feelings and actions of others.

Typically, our mother, with whom we should have been sharing our grief and who should have been comforting us and allowing us to comfort her, was intent on making this day, again, all about her and her emotions, rather than about anything or anybody else, even Dad. His wishes, despite the loving words she spoke at the graveside, were irrelevant.

I feel a pang of guilt as I write this, as it would appear as though I have no feelings of warmth or compassion for our mother. The thing is, this is farthest from the truth! All of our family have been brought up to be loving, caring, forgiving and compassionate, which is why this was all so difficult. We offered so many chances, so many reconciliations over the years, only to be left rejected and hurting all over again a few months down the line.

On the day, I continued smiling and greeting our other family members and tried to let Mum's behaviour go over my head. I did succeed in this but I do remember every bitter comment, every dig that she made and every glance that let us know that she held so much disdain for us that day. My mind was in turmoil, but I also had my children to protect and comfort too. It was a big ask but I, and my sister, did our dad proud that day. We did not respond, we did not give in to Mum's invitation to argue or show anger, but we did hurt, big time. This day of all days would have been the one when I would have liked to have seen our mum step up and be there for someone else, especially for us, her daughters, who desperately needed comfort that day.

My sister and I comforted each other though, as had become the tradition during difficult times. But over the years we have also shared so many happy times and celebrated so many special things together. All this only served to deepen the bond and the strength of our sisterly relationship.

Travelling through the woodland path, Sam the shire horse lost his footing, and we all thought the coffin was going to fly off the front of the cart. It caused several of us to have a nervous giggle, but Dad would have laughed at this too. He had a great sense of humour, so this just added to the unique memories we had to share from the day. We eventually arrived safely at the graveside, gathered to honour Dad.

Our mum read her very moving, extremely tearful, and also overdramatic poem for her 'husband' even though she had chosen to spend the last twenty-eight years apart from him. When she finished, she collapsed into someone's arms and probably never noticed the beautiful words that my son, and then my daughter, both wrote and read about their grandad. These truly were moving; they were both written and read from the heart. I can't believe how well they did and how emotional their words were and I still had to control my emotions as I was yet to read my own beautiful tribute to our dad. More than anything, I wanted to do him proud and get all my words out before I could begin to cry. I managed this and I hope I did him proud. I certainly spoke about my dad with all the passion and emotion that I held in my heart. Then, and only then, could I allow my own tears to flow. This they did in abundance as they lowered our dad's coffin into the ground to the very triumphant blasts of the trumpet solo of the 'Grand March' of *Aida*. It actually seemed fitting because Dad *was* triumphant. As all the mourners left the graveside, having thrown in their red carnations, something Dad would have loved, it suddenly dawned on me that my sister and I were the only ones remaining. There we were, his two little girls standing side by side looking down at him. Neither of us had let go of our carnations and neither of us appeared to be able to move. I know I couldn't stop thinking, 'I don't want to leave you alone like this!' We wrapped our arms around each other and comforted each other as we always did and I whispered to Jan, 'You should throw your carnation in last as you're the oldest.'

Jan whispered, 'No, you were his favourite. You should go last.' (I never knew she thought this; I certainly never thought he had a favourite.) I said, 'He loved us both the same. We should go together, on the count of three.'

So we counted, one, two, three, and together we released our carnations onto Dad's coffin, along with the words I'd written for him, then sobbed and hugged like there was no tomorrow. We stayed hugging for ages, then, slowly, hand in hand, we walked back up the woodland path to join our family and friends to celebrate Dad's life back at the woodland café on site.

There was no religious ceremony, no hype, just a simple, family-led celebration and honouring of a very, very much-loved and respected man. It was simply perfect as far as these things can be. It was all that Dad would have wanted and that is exactly what we were aiming for. So despite the family rift that had been opened wider since Dad's passing, we still achieved what we had set out to. It then made me realise that what others had previously shared about grief bringing out the best or the worst in people was actually true. I like to think that throughout this time of grieving and dealing with solicitors sending harassing letters by instruction from our mother, we still behaved with dignity, respect and compassion, as our father had taught us. This was not an easy thing to do at this difficult time!

I'd like to explain why I have included so much about my father in this book. I believe with all my heart that if I hadn't had such a lovely, nurturing and reliable father to correct the unhealthy, negative cycle of critical and abusive maternal parenting I received, then my personality, indeed my entire life, may have taken a much more destructive pathway.

When I later trained as a foster parent, I learnt so much about the impact of parental relationships on children and I began to understand how my parents had influenced me. Often children who end up in the looked-after system, do not have any positive role models in their parents. They do not receive love consistently and are not taught about healthy relationships, or how to behave in a positive and acceptable manner. Due to this they can end up with low self-worth and feel they are bad and unlovable.

Having just one parent or primary carer who corrects this by showing a child love, devotion, nurture, care and attention, in a consistent and reliable manner, can give that child a whole new outlook and positive attitude. How lucky is a child who has two such parents. I count myself lucky because I had one fantastic parent who helped to make me feel safe, offered me security and showed me the difference between a caring and a controlling relationship. He demonstrated that there was another way to behave within a healthy relationship and taught me as much about decency, morals and goodness as my Catholic education and religion did.

This is why my dad was such a powerful influence, despite his quiet yet stern outward appearance. This is why he deserves so much recognition. He helped to make decent, kind, caring citizens of myself and my sister. Both of us have worked tirelessly in our personal lives and in our careers to help others as he always did. Yet nobody really knew any of this. He didn't boast and he wasn't demonstrative; he just parented us quietly and naturally in the best way that he could. This is not to say that he was a perfect parent. I'm sure he would have said himself that parenting wasn't something he'd really thought about and he didn't feel came naturally to him, but in our experience, it did. He always responded in the best way he felt at any given moment and what he showed was commitment, devotion, love, routine, structure, boundaries and above all consistency and an unconditional love for us. I feel there isn't much more that is needed by children, and we were very lucky to have this. I am very grateful for this role model and am proud to be able to say he was my father.

23

Patty

It was nearly a full year before I saw my mother again. This only occurred because my grandmother, my mum's mother, was by now also very ill. Her health was declining rapidly. My grandma was living in a nursing home and one day it became clearly apparent to the nurses that she was no longer going to be able to sustain her life in this world. The nursing staff managed to gather my auntie, who had always been grandma's main carer, my sister and me (as her eldest granddaughters), my elder daughter and my two cousins to her bedside. We were all with Grandma when she passed away. This was certainly a blessing, as we had all remained very close and were all special in Grandma's life. What's even more important is that the local priest was also summoned, as Grandma was heavily religious. He came to her room and was able to lead us all in prayers around Grandma's bed. I found this incredibly moving and was amazed that Grandma appeared to have been holding on for a priest to arrive and pray with her and bless her. She seemed much quieter and calmer after the priest visited. Her breathing quietened and her whole body became more relaxed.

The family members sat round her bed chatting. It was difficult at times as we hadn't seen our mum since Dad's funeral and there were so many unspoken issues and tensions to resolve. I felt very uncomfortable. As Auntie Chrissie had been closest to Grandma and cared for her so well for so long leading up to this day, I felt it was important for her to be closest to Grandma at the end. Having witnessed death as a nurse, and more intimately when Dad passed, I knew the subtle signs that indicated Grandma was nearing her time. Chrissie was sat by the window. Someone made a joke about something, I forget what, but Grandma's face happened to twitch into a sort of funny little smile even though she was, by now, unconscious. I remarked that Grandma found that funny and as soon as I spoke I realised that I'd seen this before. The nurse had explained when Dad died that the last amounts of air leaving a person's lungs at the time of death often cause it to look like they are smiling, even laughing. This often gives false hope, as families see movement and hope for a miraculous healing. Anyway, I realised Grandma's time was near so I interrupted Auntie Chrissie quietly, whispering to her, 'Come, sit by Patty!' (Grandma's nickname).

Chrissie suddenly began to panic. She asked, 'Has she gone?'

I spoke quietly, took her hand and said, 'No, not yet, but come and sit here and hold her hand. It's nearly time.'

I think, and I hope, that this reassured Chrissie, and the fact that she could hold Grandma's hand, ease her fear and be close to her till the end was of some comfort. Chrissie held her hand and then placed Grandma's rosary beads in her other hand. Patty would have loved this gesture. She slipped very quietly and peacefully away surrounded by her family.

I think that when a person dies alone it must be so sad and terrifying. How lucky to be able to have one's loving family comforting you to the end. Death becomes us all. There is no avoiding it. It is the only certainty for all of us. I began to believe more and more that God intended us to use our lives well and be decent Christians, kind and caring to each other. We all hugged for what seemed ages.

24

Sjögren's Syndrome

I had recovered very well, in some ways, following my hysterectomy when I was forty-two. What happened next though, I could never have imagined. A few months after the operation, I began to suffer with extreme joint pains and aching muscles like you just can't begin to understand. It was literally excruciating. I was also so exhausted. I didn't know what was happening to me. I ached all over, all day, every day. I slept very poorly, I had a very foggy brain and I had such a dry mouth.

Most doctors assumed it was psychological, stress or emotional exhaustion. Especially when they looked at my health records and saw my previous history. I can still see it now. I'd sit in a doctor's office, explaining everything, and they'd look at their computer screen (I can imagine what they were reading) and I could see their dismissive expression as they began to think, 'It's all in her head.' Due to this, my physical health was literally dismissed for many years. Even my hysterectomy was performed, eventually, as an emergency after years of trying to explain to various doctors how ill I was. One fantastic surgeon finally believed in me and investigated. I had been complaining of gynaecological problems for eighteen years by then with no help or intervention.

When I finally went to theatre for that operation, the surgeon was horrified by the state of my insides in my lady department! He explained that in twenty-five years as a consultant gynaecologist he had never seen anything as bad. He asked me why I hadn't complained to doctors sooner. I explained that I had been trying to do exactly that for many years but that no one would believe me. Doctors be warned. Please do not disregard a person's physical symptoms just because they also have mental health conditions or previous ones. It can become dangerous, but is also, at the very least, a sad reflection of the stigma that the UK generally attaches to mental health and those afflicted by it. I am living proof that this should not be so.

After finally having my hysterectomy, I recovered from that, but was knocked down by a very mysterious illness. Again, doctors assumed it was all in my mind or stress related. I even started to believe them this time. I actually thought, 'Oh my, if my brain is psychologically capable of making me feel this much pain, then that is very scary.'

I did all that they advised. I went to physiotherapy and I learnt relaxation techniques. I also attended a pain clinic, a place, I guess, where they send you when they don't know what else to do with you. While at this clinic, I did, however, learn some very valuable lessons in pacing myself, relaxing and generally being less stressed. I also saw a wonderful psychologist, Andy, who helped me to address a few remaining issues that

I hadn't managed to deal with, namely, the grief following the loss of my father.

What didn't happen though was more remarkable. They didn't manage to help ease the pain I was experiencing on a daily basis at all. In order to be accepted by this pain clinic for treatment, I had to have exhausted all other investigations with doctors and for them to be certain there were no other existing serious conditions.

I felt convinced that I still wasn't being listened to. I felt sure something else was going on in my body. So I decided to pay for one private consultation with a rheumatologist. Imagine everyone's surprise when she very quickly (basically, immediately), established that I was, in fact, suffering from an autoimmune disorder called Sjögren's syndrome. The funny thing is, my gynaecologist had suggested months prior to this that I might be suffering from a similar autoimmune disorder, lupus, as my blood work was showing signs of this.

I was just absolutely overjoyed to learn the diagnosis, as I had begun to believe that I was actually going stark raving mad! I was also relieved to know I could now be treated with medication and physiotherapy, and although there is no cure for Sjögren's, I was now at least hopeful for some improvement.

Throughout the years of physical ill health and my divorce, my own GP had been extremely supportive. He seemed to believe I had this 'inner strength' and that I was a much nicer person than I ever dared to believe. When I told him of this diagnosis, he simply said, 'Well, if anyone can come out of this OK, then that person is you!' In fact, he continued to say, 'No, you won't just come out of this OK. You'll come out on top!'

Yet again, he had unwittingly raised my confidence and my previously very low self-esteem.

With all this in mind, at home I decided that I was fed up with being poorly. I'd already spent days, sometimes weeks and even months on end, laid up in agony in bed and, to be very honest, feeling pretty sorry for myself. I'd already been on morphine for many years, as nothing else even helped my joint pain in the slightest. Now, I realised I could at least relax, knowing that I wasn't crazy – ish – but in all seriousness that I had two options. I could sink or I could swim. I didn't want to sink. I knew I still had far more life to live, so much fun to have and many people to love, especially my children, who were, by now, growing fast into independent adulthood. I decided I wanted to be there to share in everything that life threw at us.

I now had morphine, the autoimmune medicine hydroxychloroquine, and some artificial tears and saliva for my dry eyes and mouth. Along with a few other medications, and using the pacing model to help prevent flare-ups, (there were still many), I generally began to feel much better and much more hopeful and positive about the future. I still have flare-ups and the odd bad day, but overall, I manage. I realised that this was the life I'd been dealt and we have no choice in some matters. But I wanted to enjoy life, make the very best out of it and knew that I alone had the power to write my own future, to write my next chapters for myself. I was going to make sure they were good chapters. After all, I had some very influential young adults who needed me to set them a good example in life, and I wanted to give the best example!

25

Spain

On 21 April 2012, I sat in our new apartment in Spain. My younger daughter and I moved there to find some peace for a while and, on the second anniversary of my father's funeral, I had just had the most beautiful Facebook conversation with Catherine, who, despite moving with me, was back in England for a couple of weeks to finish her college course. We had been talking about my dad, her granddad, or G-dad, as she called him. She used the term 'Brightest Star' to describe my father. It was truly beautiful, and although I wasn't writing this book at the time, I scribbled it down for future reference. We call him that to this day. I still find it hard to believe that I seem to write so well when I am emotional.

Did my mum even remember what the day was? I doubt it! She hardly ever talked about him. I still felt his loss terribly. I remember a few months after Dad passed away, I was seeing the psychologist at the pain clinic and I told him how devastated

I was at this loss and asked if I would ever get over it. I was worried, as, having worked so hard in the previous twelve years to stave off the depression, I now feared I might be headed that way again. Try as I might, I knew this would be the most difficult test yet, but I also knew that Dad would have been devastated himself if I ever succumbed to it again. For his sake, and thanks Dad, because I maybe couldn't have done it for any other reason, I rallied all my strength to keep it at bay.

My lovely psychologist, Andy, explained that I wouldn't be human if I wasn't feeling so sad at that time, but he would be more concerned if I was still feeling as sad in two years' time. I'm not sure if I had clinical depression at that moment, two years on, but what I do know is that I felt very, very sad! I think perhaps, as my GP kept telling me, I was always far too hard on myself. After all that happened, it would be pretty unusual to be feeling on top of the world, and after so many years with the physical pain I had experienced, let alone all the emotional turmoil, I suppose a certain amount of feeling low was to be expected. But I knew that I'd be dammed if I would ever let it beat me again! I wasn't going to let this develop into true depression. If I did that, I knew I'd have lost the battle, and if that happened, I wouldn't be any good to anyone. That is why I always know I have to keep strong, because I need and want to be there for a long time to come for my children, and because I won't ever let Dad down.

I also felt, at that moment, that Robert probably thought that I wasn't there for him, but I had to have a break in order to get well and strong, to be able to get back to him and continue supporting him for many years to come. Without a break, I would certainly have gone under. I had become so ill, physically and mentally, that unless I actually took time out and rested properly, I don't think I would have had the strength to fight anything. I couldn't cope with anything more.

It was so very beautiful, peaceful and tranquil in Spain. I thought I might, at last, manage to rest up a bit, but I missed my family and friends terribly. I hoped the special ones would all come and visit me there. My dog, Angel, was arriving the next day and I had been keeping in touch with her couriers as she travelled with them, via Facebook and their company blog. They posted a beautiful photo of her along the way on their website. I couldn't wait for her to arrive; she truly has been an angel to me. In Spain, her name would be something like Angelica, which we often nicknamed her anyway. She's always helped to keep me strong. I've never known such a loyal and loving four-legged friend, so sensitive to my needs and my moods. She even becomes sympathetically ill if I am. If I stayed in bed for days, she was very happy to lie there with me, almost as though she was keeping guard, or keeping watch over me. If we spent the day in bed because I didn't feel so good, every now and then she'd look up at me from the bottom of the bed, where she'd be lying across my feet, as if to say, 'You OK, Mum?' Only once I'd replied, 'It's OK, Angel. I'm all right', would she settle down again. That's a special dog!

26

Campervans, Dogs and Fostering

My time in Spain achieved what I had hoped it would. I had rested, recharged and rethought my entire future, as I was now the head of my household, with no partner or parents available to help and support me. My now adult children still depended on me a great deal, but I felt that now was my time to do the things I loved and wanted to do with my life. However, I also had to ensure that I could provide for myself and my family for many years to come.

As a family, we began to buy and enjoy Volkswagen campervans and all things VW. We also started to breed dogs with our beautiful Shetland sheepdog and this became a regular family activity as we became devoted to all our beautiful Sheltie pups. It was wonderful, making and maintaining many beautiful friendships with the new forever families that our puppies were lucky to find homes with.

The love for our dogs also prompted a career change for

my elder daughter. After studying archaeology at the University of Reading, Jennifer didn't remain in this work but found a fantastic local job as a mortgage advisor. This is not what she really wanted to do with her life, but it filled a hole for a time. After breeding dogs with me, she developed a love of working with animals and worked tirelessly as a volunteer at the RSPCA animal sanctuary in Stubbington, known as the Stubbington Ark. She applied for many full-time roles within animal care facilities and finally, after applying for an admin role in one such place, was actually offered a career path within canine hydrotherapy and research. This was an absolute dream job for Jennifer and this is what she is now pursuing.

Campervans, classic cars and Shetland sheepdogs became an everyday part of our family life, but the biggest change came as I applied for a career in foster care. This was something I had always wanted to do since first meeting my childhood best friend and her mother. She had adopted a disabled child, as well as having her own birth children, and I had always admired this lovely family. I had never felt that I was a good enough person, or mother, to be able to do this though. Having always worked in the caring profession, however, most of my job opportunities took me back to working with disabled children. This was something I loved to do. I felt the natural progression, despite my ill health, would be to offer another child, who possibly couldn't have the kind of positive childhood I had given my children, a loving and stable family life. With my improved health and with my confidence and self-esteem at a much more positive point than at any other time in life, I embarked on a long journey of assessment and training to become a foster parent.

The assessment process has been described by some as very intrusive, as the agencies need to know about your whole past in order to assess your suitability for this vocation. I understood this entirely, as we would be caring for the most vulnerable children in our society. As I had already dealt with all of my past issues in such a positive manner, especially with Chris at the Maudsley, I found the assessment process to be more cathartic than anything else. I am a very open and honest person too. I wear my heart on my sleeve and happily shared my entire life history, very proudly in a funny kind of way. There are no skeletons in my closet.

My children know everything about my life, and theirs too, so I had nothing to hide. I shared everything, and I do mean everything, with my assessor. You see, it's not that they want to trip you up or judge you if you've had a difficult or challenging life. What they really want to know about is your resilience and how you've learnt from all your past life experiences. For example, the fact that a lot of stressful things may have happened to a person is not something that they can necessarily control, but what they want to see is that these experiences have helped to make you a better and more resilient, positive person.

During my six-month assessment period, I had many visits from social workers asking all sorts of personal questions. At the end of that period, after they had talked to my four referees, I had to attend my fostering panel. The best way I can think of to describe the panel is *The X Factor* for carers!

There were about eight panel members from all areas of social care, such as a social worker, a teacher, a foster parent, a nurse and the CEO of the foster agency to name but a few, who had all read my whole assessment history. They each asked me different questions relating to foster care work. I left the room while they deliberated as to whether or not to accept me as a foster parent. I was invited back into the room and was very excited and somewhat surprised to hear that it had been a unanimous decision to accept me as a foster parent! That's like getting eight golden Xs on *The X Factor*. I was ecstatic!

My foster-care career began. I cannot divulge much about the work itself due to confidentiality and safeguarding issues. Anyone who works in social care will understand this. However, what I can share is that this is possibly the most stressful and challenging, yet rewarding role I could ever have imagined.

27

The Wedding in the Woods

The Christmas before my second granddaughter was to be born (in the March), my daughter announced that she and her boyfriend would be getting married that July. That didn't really leave much time to plan a wedding, but both my daughter and I were, by now, seasoned OCDers, which also, thankfully, made us expert organisers.

Catherine was heavily pregnant at that time so we couldn't even look at wedding dresses until after her baby was born. With just three months left until the now set wedding date, we had no dress and no venue, just our church booked for the marriage service itself. I was delighted that they had chosen to have their wedding in our family church and parish. More delighted too that my lovely friend and priest, Father Kevin, would be officiating at my daughter's marriage. I never expected that, not in a million years. Miracles do happen. I still hope and pray that one day my children will return to practising their faith alongside me in the Catholic church, the church into which they were born and baptised. I never forced religion on my children once they became old enough to make their own decisions. I do hope though that they will feel the call to return to the church, as I did.

Not only would I be paying for a great deal of the wedding, but I was also involved with the organisation, with my daughter, as well as reading during the marriage in the church and, most importantly of all, giving her away to her groom. I was deeply touched and honoured when Catherine asked me to do this. My children still had a father who could and would have done this beautiful task, but as my daughter herself explained, I had been the one to raise the children alone through their teenage years and early adult life. I had been the one consistent parental presence, caring for, providing for and loving them unconditionally through all the ups and downs of family life. She felt it was only right and fitting that I, therefore, should be the one to give her over to her new husband.

Still with no venue, Catherine was beginning to panic slightly. I happened to then visit my father's grave, situated in the beautiful sustainability site, in the natural burial ground in the heart of the South Downs. I sat on the grass by Dad's grave, chatting away to him as though he was sat beside me. I often do this. I even explained the dilemma of having no wedding venue. I wasn't expecting an answer in the true sense of the word, but as I walked back through the woods to the car park, my eyes were drawn to the wooded teaching/events venue, which had been recently built to host functions on the site. It was wooden, open and rustic. I was so impressed by the simplicity of this building and how it appeared to have a kind of natural beauty and was surrounded by beautiful woodland.

I found myself thinking that Dad himself may have found us a wedding venue. I thought this would be a perfect setting for a very unusual yet personal wedding, as it could be dressed in any way we chose yet remained beautiful in its own natural setting. I didn't think Catherine and her boyfriend would agree, but thought I'd mention it to them anyway. I was astounded when they both agreed that this was a perfect venue for the type of wedding they were planning. Thank you, Dad!

The other role I was to play that day was one of chauffeur to the bride on the way to her wedding and then also to deliver the newly married couple to their venue to celebrate with family and friends. The reason for this role was so that Catherine could go to her wedding in her chosen, favourite form of transport, namely our own VW campervan, Patricia.

I had recently acquired Patricia, our second family campervan. I had used our first to deliver Catherine to her prom during the last year of school and it seemed right and fitting for us to drive together in our second one on her wedding day. Patricia had other ideas. After a test drive the evening before, Patricia broke down, big time. You could say, her big end had bust!

Patricia was an automatic camper so she couldn't even be towed away. I watched, sobbing, as my beautiful Patricia was driven off into the sunset on the back of a lorry. As she disappeared on the horizon, so too did our hopes of driving to the wedding together in our own classic vehicle. It then dawned on me that it was, by now, late evening the night before the wedding and we had no transport for the bride. A fantastic local company, Vinnie's Vintage Vehicles, came to the rescue and was able to drive me and Catherine to her wedding at very short notice, in a much smarter VW campervan than ours. This was a true wedding vehicle. In a way, this was much nicer for me too. I was already doing so much at the wedding and to be able to actually sit back and enjoy the ride to the wedding with my daughter, properly together, holding her hand and reassuring her, was far more enjoyable. I sat back, relaxed for bit and simply enjoyed the ride!

I could not have been a prouder mother, or person, as I walked my daughter down the aisle in my own parish church where I had worked and volunteered and was, I hope, a valued member of the community. Catherine and her husband chose not to have a choir, which, initially, I was a little upset about as I love hymns and even sang in the choir. They stripped the service back to the simplest and barest parts of the wedding service and chose their own, very beautiful music to be played at specific times, namely, walking down the aisle, during the signing of the register and walking back down the aisle once officially married. I must say though, in this simplest and most basic of forms, they had actually achieved a most beautiful wedding service that was commented upon by many of our own parishioners who attended. Even Father Kevin, who was to leave our parish soon after this, mentioned how their chosen simple ceremony had actually been extremely moving and powerful as they had removed what was not really necessary and concentrated on the essential, true meaning of marriage.

The wedding in the woods was beautiful. Very, very different and very, very natural and wonderful.

28

Grandchildren

Despite raising my son as normally as I possibly could, even though he had been diagnosed with autism, ADHD and learning difficulties, and despite always encouraging him, saying he could achieve anything he wanted in life, just like anybody else, there were still, secretly, two things I thought that he would probably never achieve. I should not have doubted him and I should have believed more strongly in his character; after all, I raised him well, I think. For this, I owe him a massive apology.

Anyway, very quietly and secretly, there were two things I thought he would never do: drive and have a relationship and family. And he has both.

He was lucky enough to meet two lovely girls actually. His first girlfriend, I hope he won't mind me sharing, came along just after my father passed away. This relationship lasted a few months. Robert was literally broken-hearted when it ended. He grieved for his grandad and he grieved for his first love. He then met another girl and, well, you know, one thing led to another and all of sudden my wonderful son was announcing to me that they were having a baby. It's kind of funny how he told me.

He knew how I loved my religion and that the sanctity of marriage and the family were still things I held in high regard. He thought I might be cross. While it would have been nicer to have had a baby within a marriage, I understand that things are very different for our young adults these days. I'm still not saying that it's OK, but I also feel that life, any life, is a blessing.

Robert and his girlfriend had stayed over at my house, as they did once every week, as they were living together mostly at her parent's home, and early in the morning I was using the bathroom when Robert shouted out, 'Mum, are you busy? It's just that we have something we need to tell you!'

I said something along the lines of, 'Well, sort of, I'm having a wash', but I rushed and joined them in the lounge.

Robert blurted out, 'We're going to have a baby!'

I love children and, like I said, life is a blessing. I burst into tears of joy. That was my spontaneous, natural response to this news. I was really overjoyed that we'd be welcoming a little person, a lovely little baby, to our family. Secretly, I was pleasantly surprised too, as this was something that I thought perhaps Robert would never experience and I had always felt sad about it.

When I told other family members later that I was going to be a nanny and they tried to guess which of my children this was related to, they too were pleasantly surprised. So it was, in September 2013, that I became a nanny to a beautiful baby girl. I love being a nanny!

I wish I could say that this was a happy ever after, but life isn't always too rosy, as we know. Robert and his girlfriend parted when their daughter was two years old. My little granddaughter, like her father, was also diagnosed with complex additional needs in all areas of her development.

When they first parted, Robert returned to live at home with me. I was, by now, a fully fledged foster mummy with other little ones living in my home. My granddaughter stayed over at ours for three nights each week. I adored her. It wasn't always easy, but love usually finds a way.

Two years later, I became a nanny again, to another gorgeous little girl. This was also a surprise. She was born to my younger daughter, Catherine, who delivered this news in a somewhat unusual way. She, too, was living with her boyfriend at that time (who later became her husband), and had come to visit me, stating that she had a present for me. I was rather bemused by all this as she passed me her handbag and said I was to search for my present inside. I couldn't find any present and said this to her. She merely said, 'Keep rummaging. You'll find something!'

As I searched again, my hands discovered an unusual-shaped object, which I removed from the bag. I lifted the item, discovering it was a pregnancy test, a used pregnancy test with a positive reading noted on the front! As I looked at Catherine, she just nodded and smiled. Once again, I was reduced to tears of joy. This little baby girl was also going to be delivered with me in attendance as one of her mummy's birthing partners. I was delighted by this invitation. It was a truly magnificent experience helping my daughter labour and being present as my granddaughter was born. My daughter was so exhausted immediately after the birth that she didn't even have any strength left in her arms to hold her baby girl, so I was more than happy to step in here. I sat in the rocking chair with my new baby granddaughter for four hours, just rocking and looking lovingly into her beautiful eyes while her mummy recovered. I wanted to savour this moment for as long as I could. This was a moment I was not going to rush. We just rocked back and forth and she gazed back up at my face lovingly too. I never thought I could ever love another child, or children, as I did my own, but when I held my granddaughters that view changed dramatically.

Epilogue

So, what of life now? Well, all of life is a constant, changing journey, with many twists and turns. You never know what's going to happen next. What I do know is, I love life. There is so much joy in watching my children and grandchildren grow. So much joy in the wisdom that comes with age and the realisation of how rich our lives are, or can be, and I don't mean monetary wealth. I'll never be rich in that sense, but I am content with my lovely family, my friends, my job and my situation. I am rich in blessings. I am rich in happiness. That doesn't mean that all is perfect and there's never a bad day, far from it. Challenges jump up from around a corner or behind a bush frequently, when you least expect it. But generally, I've found a peacefulness that comes with acceptance and love. Acceptance of our life path and of our challenges and acceptance of each other and ourselves. That's quite hard to achieve, especially with the things life throws at us, but I've worked hard on me to achieve this. I know me well now, the me that's evolved through all these life situations and now, I'm comfortable with me! I do have to say that I also have great faith in my religion and my relationship with the church has helped me enormously to achieve this.

My whole life recently took on another great change and prompted a return to my previous career. As a young student nurse, before marriage and children, I dreamed of becoming a paediatric nurse. That all changed when my own family arrived earlier than I had anticipated. I don't regret for one minute that they did and I wanted to champion the cause for full-time devoted motherhood, which I did, and I'm proud to have done so. Now my children are grown, with children of their own, and I've been very fortunate to have been offered a senior healthcare assistant role in paediatrics. I know I am very lucky and may even be able to return fully to nursing practice within this wonderful specialty, if I play my cards right!

There are still difficulties to overcome. I have grandchildren with additional needs, and fosterlings, also with additional needs. I have an ageing dog. I don't have the very best of health and recently even broke my wrist just after starting my new job, completely out of the blue, but that's life. Sometimes life messes up a bit. Mostly we can overcome these things and when we see the world, our lives, in fact, all of creation, surely, we have to marvel at this and be grateful for what we have.

I am blessed, I know that. The not-so-good bits, I'm still working on. I have a relationship with my mother now that works at my pace, my rules, which I can manage. That way everyone wins. If we choose not to forgive others their wrongdoings then we are no better than them, and we harbour nothing but resentment and regret if we do so. Isn't there a saying, to err is human, to forgive is divine? Forgiveness isn't a weak characteristic. Forgiveness often takes great strength, but it reaps far greater rewards. We should all be a little more forgiving and a little more tolerant in this very stressful thing they call life!

If reading my book helps one other person to overcome or deal better with their own mental health difficulties or life challenges, then for me it will have been a job well done! I truly hope it helps.

For OCDers, those with depression, anxiety or any other difficulty related to mental health, remember, you are far from alone. This is an illness of the brain, just as any other person can have an illness of any other body organ. One in four people will suffer with some form of mental health illness, more than any of the other body organs. It is time for the stigma attached to mental health difficulties to be banished from our society. It is discrimination of huge proportion!

Be brave, be strong and be well.

For my family xxxxxxxx

Medical conditions

Autism

Autism is a developmental disorder, which is characterised by difficulties with social interactions and communication. People with autism have repetitive and restricted behaviour patterns.

Characteristics of their differences in communication style, interpersonal relationships and social interactions are not limited to one setting. They occur for the individual in different environments. This can include being non-verbal or having unusual speech patterns and having difficulty understanding non-verbal communication cues. People with autism often find it more difficult to build and maintain friendships and to hold typical back-and-forth conversations. Speech patterns may be monotone with repetitive sounds or phrases and echolalia (this is when a person repeats back what has just been said to them).

There is a dislike of changes in routine and transitions are often difficult for those on the spectrum of autism.

Autism is a spectrum disorder as it can range from mild to severe. Those with autistic spectrum disorders can also have very intense, restricted interests and can be extremely sensitive to any or many of the various sensory stimuli. They can be oversensitive or less sensitive to light, sound, taste or touch.

Autism can also produce extreme anxiety in those affected and can come with meltdowns and/or shutdowns. Parenting autistic children is both challenging and extremely rewarding. They have an abundance of positive attributes.

For advice and support:

- National Autistic Society, www.autism.org.uk
- Autism Speaks, www.autismspeaks.org
- Mencap, www.mencap.org.uk
- Scope, www.scope.org.uk

Attention deficit and hyperactivity disorder (ADHD)

ADHD is a condition that includes symptoms such as inattentiveness, hyperactivity and impulsive behaviour. This can include a short attention span, constantly fidgeting and acting without thinking, often without regard for danger.

ADHD can be treated with medication and/or talking therapies.

It is not clear what causes ADHD, but two things are certain: first, it is strongly hereditary, and second, it is a biological condition. The behaviour and learning problems associated with ADHD are caused by subtle differences in the fine-tuning of the brain.

In the past, ADHD has been blamed on poor parenting or even diet. It is now recognised by the medical profession as a biological difference in the brain.

For advice and support:

- ADHD Foundation, www.adhdfoundation.org.uk
- Scope, www.scope.org.uk
- The Challenging Behaviour Foundation, www.challengingbehaviour.org.uk

Obsessive Compulsive Disorder (OCD)

OCD is an anxiety-based disorder that has two main parts: obsessions and compulsions.

Obsessions are unwelcome intrusive thoughts, worries, doubts or even images that repeatedly come into the mind and cannot seem to be budged. They are based on fear and/or anxiety and yet can make you feel more anxious, resulting in a perpetual negative cycle.

Compulsions are repetitive actions that you do to rid yourself of the anxiety and the ruminations this causes. The compulsion could be something like repeatedly checking doors, locks or the cooker, or it might be repeating a specific phrase in your head. Many people with OCD will perform washing rituals, such as repetitive hand-washing to rid themselves of a fear such as dirt or germs.

It is not just about being tidy! It is about having no control over completely irrational, negative thoughts. It's about being very afraid that if you don't do things a certain way then something bad or harmful will happen.

Sometimes symptoms of OCD may seem better controlled while at other times they can make day-to-day life really difficult. They can be more exaggerated during times of stress.

OCD can have a major impact on the way some people live their lives. Repeating compulsions can take up an enormous amount of time. You may even feel an overwhelming need to avoid certain places or situations. It can impact on work, home life and relationships. Some people with OCD are not able to shop, eat out at restaurants, use public transport or even go outside. OCD can also make you feel isolated, lonely and ashamed. Many people try to hide their OCD from those closest to them and from others.

The feeling of anxiety that is both a cause and a result of OCD can make you become a slave to the compulsions as you feel you have to carry them out so frequently and have no control over them.

OCD can be treated with medication and/or talking therapies. Cognitive behavioural therapy can be of great benefit. It certainly was in my case.

For advice and support:

- OCD UK, www.ocduk.org
- Mind, a mental health charity, www.mind.org.uk
- Mental Health Foundation, www.mentalhealth.org.uk
- Maudsley Charity, SLaM (South London and Maudsley NHS Foundation Trust, SLaM), www.slam.nhs.uk

Sjögren's Syndrome

Sjögren's syndrome is named after the Swedish doctor who first described it. Sjögren's is a systemic, chronic progressive autoimmune disease that affects the entire body. Along with symptoms of dryness that affect any moisture-producing organ or gland in the body, there are other serious complications such as fatigue, chronic pain, major organ involvement and lymphomas.

Most patients experience dry eyes, dry mouth, fatigue and joint pain. Sjögren's can also cause dysfunction of other organs and body systems, such as the kidneys, gastrointestinal system, blood vessels, lungs, heart, liver, pancreas and central nervous system. People with Sjögren's syndrome also have a higher chance of developing lymphoma (cancer of the lymphatic system).

No two people with Sjögren's will have the same symptoms. Each person will have different symptoms and these can be mild or severe and may even disappear at times. There are relapses (flare-ups) and remissions (periods of time when symptoms are very mild or have gone away). The disease can affect different body systems in different people but can also change to include more body systems or organs in an individual as the disease progresses.

Some symptoms experienced could include:

- Dry eyes
- Dry mouth, mouth sores, dental decay, difficulty chewing or swallowing
- Dry nose, nose bleeds, sinusitis
- Neurological problems, such as poor memory or headaches
- Change of smell or taste
- Dry lips
- Dry throat
- Swollen and painful parotid or salivary glands
- Heartburn or reflux
- Recurrent bronchitis, pneumonia, pleurisy
- Breathlessness, respiratory issues, cough
- Stomach upsets, Irritable Bowel Syndrome, autoimmune pancreatitis

- Abnormal liver function tests, autoimmune hepatitis
- Arthritis, joint/muscle pain
- Peripheral neuropathy
- Vaginal dryness
- Fatigue, vasculitis, lymphoma
- Brain fog
- Skin sensitivity to UV light

Treatments can involve medication, pacing activities and physiotherapy. Medications can be non-steroidal anti-inflammatory drugs, steroids, disease-modifying antirheumatic drugs and many more. Artificial tears and artificial saliva sprays are also beneficial for dry eyes and mouth.

For advice and support:

- The British Sjögren's Syndrome Association, www.bssa.uk.net
- Sjögren's Foundation, www.sjogrens.org
- Versus Arthritis, www.versusarthritis.org
- Lupus UK, www.lupusuk.org.uk
- Lupus Foundation of America, www.lupus.org

This section is based on my own experience and understanding of these conditions and readers should consult their own doctors with concerns.

CPSIA information can be obtained
at www.ICGtesting.com
Printed in the USA
LVHW090813240122
709011LV00003BA/70